THREE PLAYS

THE COURTYARD OF WONDERS
THE FOUR LEGS OF THE TABLE
IBSENLAND

MARJORIE CHAMBERS was born in Northern Ireland and educated at Trinity College Dublin and the Sorbonne. She taught Modern Greek Language and Literature at Queen's University Belfast. Her translations of Greek poetry, prose and drama have been published in the U.S.A., Greece, England and the Republic of Ireland, and, apart from the plays of Kambanellis (for which, see the Copyright page), they include the following:

Kalamos and Acheron, a collection of short stories by Christoforos Milionis (Kedros Publishers, Athens 1990).

Prison Poems by Yannis Ritsos (The Goldsmith Press, Newbridge, Co. Kildare, Ireland, 2001).

My Life in the Furnace by Panayotis Tranoulis (Pella Publishing, New York, 2005).

Poems by Yannis Ritsos in *The Charioteer* 29/30 (1987/88) and *Modern Greek Studies Yearbook* 7 (1991); by George Vafopoulos in *The Charioteer* 31/32 (1989/90); by Nikiforos Vrettakos in *The Charioteer* 33/34 (1991/92); by Nikos Gatsos in *The Charioteer* 36 (1995/96); by Miltos Sachtouris in *The Charioteer* 37/38 (1997/99); and by Yannis Kondos in *Stand* NS 1.3 (1999).

She has also published critical articles on some of the Greek authors she has translated:

"Ritsos in Belfast" in *Themata Logotechnias* [*Literary Matters*] 5 (March–June 1997).

"Translating Millionis" in *Themata Logotechnias* 23 (May–August 2003).

'Ritsos and Greek mythology" in *Hermathena: A Trinity College Dublin Review* 153 (1992); republished in *Themata Logotechnias* 42 (2009).

IAKOVOS KAMBANELLIS

THREE PLAYS

The Courtyard of Wonders

The Four Legs of the Table

Ibsenland

TRANSLATED FROM THE GREEK BY
MARJORIE CHAMBERS

COLENSO BOOKS
2015

This edition of the *Three Plays* first published by Colenso Books 2015

Colenso Books
68 Palatine Road, London N16 8ST, UK
colensobooks@gmail.com

The Introduction and translations © Marjorie Chambers 2015

ISBN 978-0-9928632-2-7

The Courtyard of Wonders was first published by Kedros Publishers
(Athens) as *Η αυλή των θαυμάτων* © Iakovos Kambanellis 1978.
This translation is published here for the first time with the agreement of
Katerina Kambanelli and Kedros Publishers.

The Four Legs of the Table was first published by Kedros Publishers
(Athens) as *Τα τέσσερα πόδια του τραπεζιού*
© Iakovos Kambanellis 1981.
This translation was first published in 1996 in *Modern International Drama* 29.2 and is republished with the agreement of Binghamton University, State University of New York, Binghamton, NY.

Ibsenland was first published by Kedros Publishers (Athens)
as *Στη χώρα Ιψεν* © Iakovos Kambanellis 1994.
This translation was first published in *Greek Letters* 14 (2000/01)
and is republished with the agreement of *Greek Letters* (Athens).

The three articles by Louis Muinzer which constitute the Appendix
were first published in Greek translation in *Θέματα Λογοτεχνίας* (1996
and 2005), and are published here for the first tme in the original English
with the agreement of Betsy Muinzer and Christos Alexiou (on behalf of
Θέματα Λογοτεχνίας, Athens) © Betsy Muinzer 2015.

The cover shows a scene from a Greek production of *The Courtyard of Wonders* at the Sarakinado Theatre, Zakynthos, March–April 2015.

Enquiries about performance rights should be directed in the first instance
to Colenso Books, who can reformat the electronic files to your
requirements to produce performance texts of any of the plays.
The translator can advise on songs where these occur
in *The Courtyard of Wonders* and *The Four Legs of the Table*
and provide recordings or sheet music.

Printed and bound in Great Britain by
Lightning Source UK Ltd
Chapter House, Pitfield, Kiln Farm,
Milton Keynes MK11 3LW

CONTENTS

Introduction by Marjorie Chambers	vii
The Courtyard of Wonders	1
Foreword by Iakovos Kambanellis (1957)	3
Foreword by Iakovos Kambanellis (1975)	5
The characters in the play	7
A note on the pronunciation of names	8
Act One	9
Act Two	28
Act Three	43
Act Four	64
The Four Legs of the Table	79
Foreword by Iakovos Kambanellis	81
The characters in the play	83
A note on the pronunciation of names	84
Act One, Scene One	85
Act One, Scene Two	94
Act Two	110
Ibsenland	137
Foreword by Iakovos Kambanellis	139
Ibsenland	141
Appendix: Three articles by Louis Muinzer	183
Kambanellis in Belfast	
(on *The Four Legs of the Table*)	185
A Kambanellis playreading in Belfast	
(on *Ibsenland*)	189
Kampanellis visits Ibsen	
(on *Ibsenland* performed in Oslo)	193

INTRODUCTION

IAKOVOS KAMBANELLIS: A BIOGRAPHICAL NOTE

Iakovos Kambanellis was born in Naxos in 1921, one of nine children. When his father had to close his pharmacy, and was unable to find suitable employment, he moved the family to Athens in 1935.

After finishing at the Sivitanidios Technical School in 1938, Iakovos found a job as a draughtsman. During the German Occupation of Greece, he and a friend were attempting, with false passports, to reach Switzerland via Austria, but when they arrived in Vienna, the friend decided not to continue the journey. Kambanellis was then arrested in Innsbruck as a vagrant and sent to Mauthausen concentration camp.

After his release from Mauthausen in 1945, he followed up his childhood interest in the theatre, and went on to become Greece's most distinguished dramatist. He wrote a dozen full-length plays, as well as several one-act plays and several film scripts. His work has been performed in many countries, including Bulgaria, Germany, Italy, Norway, Romania, Sweden, Turkey and the U.S.A.

The "Father of Greek Drama", as Kambanellis is known in Greece, was successful in introducing, under the influence of the innovative director Karolos Koun, a social realism more appropriate to the post-war years than the middle-class comedies hitherto popular. However, his talent was regarded with suspicion during the rule of the Junta (1967–74). In 1973, when the students occupied the Athens Polytechnic, Kambanellis's anti-dictatorship play *Our Big Circus* was produced at the open-air Athineon Theatre. Attempts were made by the authorities to censor a number of scenes — to no avail, despite the intimidating presence of the Junta police staring fixedly at the audience. As a result of this production, though, Kambanellis was placed under house arrest, until the fall of the Junta in the following year.

In 1981, he accepted an invitation to head the Hellenic Broadcasting Corporation, but six years later he gave up this post and returned to writing and directing.

After forty years of renowned success as a playwright, the Arts Theatre, where many of his plays had been performed, honoured him in 1990 by producing his *Odysseus Come Home* in the ancient

INTRODUCTION

theatre of Herod Atticus in Athens. This was the first time a modern play had been included in the Athens Festival programme; and it marked the beginning of the proper recognition of Kambanellis's contribution to the arts. In 1995, he was made Honorary Doctor of the School of Philosophy, University of Cyprus; in 1998, and 1999, honorary doctorates were conferred upon him by the Departments of Theatre Studies in the universities of Thessaloniki and Athens, and then, in 1999 — the highest accolade of all — he was elected a member of the Academy of Athens.

In the years that followed, his plays continued to be produced, notably in Washington, in Ankara, and in Florence, where *The Courtyard of Wonders* was presented in Italian by the Lemon Tree Theatre.

Iakovos Kampanellis died in March 2011 at the age of eighty-nine.

THE COURTYARD OF WONDERS

When Kambanellis returned to Greece, having survived imprisonment in Mauthausen, he found a country physically devastated and emotionally traumatised, following the German Occupation and the Civil War. Throughout the decade that followed, Athens was being rebuilt to house the huge influx of refugees from the country areas, where property and livelihood had been destroyed during the Civil War. The small houses lining the streets of Athens gave way to large blocks of flats.

For six months, the playwright lived in an apartment block overlooking a yard encircled by single-storey houses — a common feature in working class areas. During this time, he observed strong feelings of community among the inhabitants — a way of life that was very soon to disappear. *The Courtyard of Wonders*, which was prompted by this experience, was first produced in 1957 at the Arts Theatre in Athens.

On top of their insecurity with regard to the threat of displacement, the characters in *The Courtyard* also face serious economic uncertainty. They are not poverty-stricken, but any employment that can be found tends to be part-time and insecure.

Their anxiety expresses itself in a longing to escape, which they attempt to do in various ways: Stelios borrows money to gamble; Anneto rents out her apartment to spend a year in Paros with

INTRODUCTION

relatives; Jordan creates a refuge for himself on the roof of his house where he can drink and daydream in peace; and Babis and Voula try to emigrate to Australia where they believe they will quickly achieve financial security.

Inevitably, the contractors come to measure the yard for a new block of flats. The "wonders" of this courtyard relate to the solidarity among the characters and the courage they show when they have to leave the yard, facing the destruction of their little community. However, although the scene is deeply moving, there is no sentimentality in the portrayal of this traumatic event. Jordan, who as a refugee from Asia Minor in 1922 has already been displaced, refuses to come down from his refuge. When at last he does agree, he grasps the handles of his handcart and leads the inhabitants out from the yard, to go their separate ways, into a future that appears uncertain.

THE FOUR LEGS OF THE TABLE

For the first time in his repertoire Iakovos Kambanellis considers, in *The Four Legs of the Table*, the positon of the upper middle class and the perception they have of their role in a capitalist society.

In conversation with me in 1994 Iakovos remarked that the play is a satire rather than a comedy. When I asked how rich exactly was the upper middle class in Greece he assured me that they were "fabulously rich" with original paintings on the walls of their houses. Later he was pleased to know that the audience, at a subsequent rehearsed reading of the play in Belfast, found the struggle among the siblings for dominance in the firm very amusing — especially when the masks of politeness slip and their language becomes less than refined.

However, the ultimate quarrel culminates in distressing revelations to one another about their children, who in various ways have betrayed their class, thus removing any guarantee of wealth and political influence in the future.

The father's detailed autobiographical account of how the firm was created, read aloud to the siblings by Alice, is a significant comment on the socio-political state of the country. The old man is frank about how he cheated and manipulated and acquired government loans to achieve his wealth. The siblings are not particularly affected by such details; what mortifies them are the references to their father's very modest background, the fact that he came upon the recipe for his famous brandy by chance, and also his taste in music which places him firmly in the peasant class. Yet, despite their disapproval of his favourite song "Speak to me Birbili", the siblings find themselves dancing enthusiastically to this very tune around their father's bed on his birthday, thus inadvertently betraying their family's humble origins.

The father's advice, in his account, that his heirs should stick together so that the firm will continue to thrive and develop is immediately ignored when they start quarrelling again. However, his wish is ironically fulfilled when, in the end, they do come together — but looking to the past rather than to the future. Iakovos also remarked to me that the last lines of the play convey the opinion that the Greeks are unable to create their own future. They don't move forward; they stand still. The old man is the table — an ironic symbol of the dynamism of yesteryear. The four sons are the legs of the table — standing guard at the four corners of a tomb.

A rehearsed reading of the present translation took place at the Lyric Theatre, Belfast in May 1995.

IBSENLAND

In 1881, no Scandinavian theatre would produce Ibsen's *Ghosts*. There was moral outrage at the criticism in the play of an inherited, overblown sense of duty that will inevitably crush "the joy of living", as Osvald expresses it. This sense of duty is urged upon Helena by the pompous and self-righteous Pastor Manders, who denies his love for her, and so condemns her to a deeply unhappy marriage to Captain Alving, a man he knows to be dissolute.

In *Ibsenland*, which was first produced in 1995, Kambanellis explores the flawed character of Manders. At the root of his behaviour are his feelings of social inferiority. His compensating and overweening ambition is to become an exceptional pastor, a goal which, in his view, demands celibacy. He persuades Helena that the physical aspect of marriage will not affect her purity of spirit, provided she exercises control over her physical desire. In this way, she can preserve her superior nature and the sanctity of marriage (and he can continue to idolise her and maintain her love for him). Soon after her marriage, as in *Ghosts*, Helena flees from her husband. Throwing herself on the mercy of Manders, she

INTRODUCTION

describes the physical aspect of her marriage and her failure to curb her own sexual desires with a frankness that Ibsen could not have dared to employ. Even more shocked and disillusioned than he appears in *Ghosts*, Manders sends her away.

The next significant scene, as in *Ghosts*, involves a meeting between Manders and Mrs Alving, now widowed. Manders, knowing the character of the late husband, is taken aback when he hears that she will name the orphanage she is about to found after her husband and not after a saint. She also insists, through clever and bitter arguments, that Manders will be President of the new orphanage. Here, Kambanellis manages to arouse a greater sympathy for Manders, in view of Mrs Alving's coldly adroit handling of the interview.

There follows a moving scene between Manders and Helena's son Osvald, who is soon to die of syphilis, a disease inherited from his father. Manders is profoundly unsettled by the young man's probing questions about his parents' strange and unhappy marriage.

The final scene is a Chekovian encounter between Manders and Mrs Alving. Their fragmented conversation is a moving epilogue to a deeply sad story of unfulfilled love, of loneliness and wasted lives.

This final scene was added for the present translation. I felt very honoured when Iakovos invited me to choose the trees and the birds; I chose "birch trees" and "geese" as being appropriately Nordic, the geese also evoking the melancholy tone of the encounter.

Rehearsed readings of this translation of *Ibsenland* took place at the Lyric Theatre, Belfast in May 1998, and at the Writers' Centre, Washington, DC in January 2001; and the translation was a subject for study at the Actors' Studio, New York, in the autumn of 2000.

FURTHER READING

As a companion to *Ibsenland* I would recommend Peter Watts's translation of *Ghosts* in *Ghosts and Other Plays* by Henrik Ibsen (Harmondsworth: Penguin, 1964).

Mauthausen by Iakovos Kambanellis, translated into English by Gail Holst-Warhaft (Athens: Kedros, *c.* 1995) is a memoir of the author's experience in the Mauthausen concentration camp.

An insight into the political and literary climate in which

INTRODUCTION

Kambanellis lived and wrote can be found in *Greece without Columns* by David Holden (London: Faber, 1972) and in *Background to Contemporary Greece*, a collection of essays on history and culture, edited in two volumes by Marion Sarafis and Martin Eve (London: Merlin Press, 1990).

ACKNOWLEDGEMENTS

I am indebted to my son Michael Chambers for his careful reading of the scripts and his very helpful advice on dialogue; and to Michelle McGaughey for her speedy and efficient retyping of the texts in the electronic format required by the publisher. I remember with gratitude the late Dr Louis Muinzer who encouraged me to translate Greek drama and presented, with his Delphic Players, the rehearsed readings mentioned above of *The Four Legs of the Table* and *Ibsenland* at the Lyric Theatre, Belfast. The readings are the subject of two of the three short articles by Dr Muinzer which make up the Appendix to the present volume.

I am grateful to the author's daughter, Katerina Kambanelli, for kindly allowing the publication or republication of these translations. And not least, I remember with gratitude the late Iakovos Kambanellis himself, who so readily and kindly responded to my questions.

MARJORIE CHAMBERS
Holywood, Co. Down, 2015

THE COURTYARD

OF WONDERS

FOREWORD

TO

THE COURTYARD OF WONDERS

PRODUCED AT THE ARTS THEATRE, ATHENS, 1957–58

If anyone asked me what, as a writer, I wanted to achieve in the theatre, I would reply: "To write plays whose origin would be, as genuinely as possible, rooted in the social and cultural values of our country." And if anyone asked me what my ambition in the theatre was, I would say that I wanted, in a series of plays, to discover the characteristics of the people of our country and in our time, through the transitory expression of their relationship with the social reality of today.

The Courtyard of Wonders is based on the lack of stability and security which characterises the life of a Greek. This instability, so familiar to all of us, begins with our changeable weather, our "strategic" geographical position, and the poverty of our country — and ends with our own economy. Everything in Greece fluctuates very easily — flows along, and then disappears. And so the habitual longing of the Greek is to consolidate himself somewhere, to make *something* secure.

The working class always expresses with more authenticity life's characteristics. Because of this it is not by chance that I have set my play in the realm of the working class.

The fluidity of conditions in the life of a Greek, the Mediterranean temperament, an ingrained resistance to difficulties, and an optimism shape a character which does not have solid boundaries; you cannot easily define him. In the same individual you see the most contradictory feelings being born, which run the whole gamut from good to bad — and, conversely, you see a continuous revelation of spiritual resources, a series of small miracles.

In *The Courtyard of Wonders* I tried not to stop at the outward expression of the relationship between man and his social environment. I tried, perhaps more profoundly, to see *how* this factor compels the specific person, the Greek, to function as an interior mechanism. I based my play on a myth that would present me with outward appearances, typical characteristics of coherence, but in a sequence of simple everyday occurrences which comprise a picture of Greek reality; and within these occurrences I tried to find whatever is a permanent and basic element of life.

Accordingly, I wanted the characters with their everyday, apparently unimportant reactions — which would place them clearly in our recent past — to reveal the more universal human being.

When writing this foreword it was not my intention to present a definitive analysis of my play. I have tried to explain the core of my objectives, so as to make it easier for the audience to see more clearly what the writer has added.

IAKOVOS KAMBANELLIS

FOREWORD

TO

THE COURTYARD OF WONDERS

PRODUCED AT THE THESSALIKO THEATRE, LARISSA, 1975–76

The decade of the 1950s and beyond was a period of great economic and social unrest, agreements, and divisions. The enormous damage that the calamity of war had inflicted on us, the political unrest, and the psychological disintegration which followed the Civil War, kept the country with its wounds open throughout the decade of the forties. Because of this, we entered the post-war era in a profoundly backward state, not only in time but also with disparate preconceptions concerning the evolutionary needs of the people.

Reorganisation, reconstruction, manufacturing, and trade did indeed quickly begin to develop. Year by year life was rapidly changing its aspect. But the change was not equally generous to all of the social classes. Political passions, phobias, and especially the exploitation of these, were preventing a more just and less unequal distribution of the wealth that economic progress was bringing. The income gap between the manual and white collar workers and the shrewd "businessman" involved in reconstruction, or the industrialist supported by loans, the merchant, the ship-owner etc. was markedly wider than it had been before the war. The distance from the thriving centre of Athens to her neighbourhoods with their unpaved roads, the refugee settlements and densely populated courtyards, became even greater. In these yards, which pre-war naivety had sprinkled with an idyllic and romantic aura, life in reality was a very harsh story of abundant squalor.

In these neighbourhoods and courtyards the better life that reorganisation and reconstruction was creating was very slow to arrive. The share of the economic miracle for the impoverished citizens who lived there, was nothing more than a low wage, with no certainty of employment. Here reigned insecurity, and escape into petty sentimentalism and daydreaming. The people in the courtyard of the play that you are about to see have been left stranded, unprotected even from themselves, sunk into habits and a way of life that do not help them to see the face of God. For this reason the biggest changes that come to them are the yearning for emigration, and the reality of the bulldozer which levelled the courtyards for redevelopment. *The Courtyard of Wonders*, when I wrote it, was the swansong of a world profoundly ours and profoundly embittered.

IAKOVOS KAMBANELLIS

THE COURTYARD OF WONDERS

A play in four acts, with a single interval between Act Two and Act Three.

THE CHARACTERS IN THE PLAY

BABIS:	Employment unspecified, husband of Voula.
VOULA:	Wife of Babis.
MARIA:	Sometimes referred to as Maritsa. Her husband, who works as stoker on ships, is absent.
JORDAN:	A refugee from Asia Minor, the husband of Asta.
ASTA:	Wife of Jordan.
YANNIS:	Son of Jordan and Asta.
ANNETO:	Widow, over sixty years old, with a daughter in England.
DORA:	A young unmarried girl.
STRATOS:	A newcomer, who rents a room from Anneto, and has an affair with Olga.
STELIOS:	A clerk, husband of Olga ("Stilianos" in Act Four).
OLGA:	Wife of Stelios, and in love with Stratos.

SURVEYOR A (Acts Two and Four only)

SURVEYOR B (Acts Two and Four only)

POSTMAN (Act Four only)

POLICEMAN (Act Four only)

MAN (Act One only)

YOUNG MAN (Act Four only)

VOICE (Act Four only)

In the dialogue the vocative forms of the male character's names occur frequently: Babi, Yanni, Strato, Stelio.

A NOTE ON THE PRONUNCIATION OF NAMES

The names of the characters Anneto and Asta are both stressed on the final syllable: An-ne-*to*, As-*ta*. Other personal and place names in the text of the play where the position of the stress may not be obvious are:

Apostolos	A-*pos*-to-los
Asian	A-si-*an*
Athena	A-*the*-na (street named after the goddess, English pronunciation)
Chrisoula	Chri-*sou*-la
Faliron	*Fa*-li-ron
Kiriakos	Ki-ri-*a*-kos
Malamatas	Ma-la-ma-*tas*
Maritsa	Ma-*ri*-tsa
Misiri	Mi-*si*-ri
Stavros	*Stav*-ros
Stelios	*Ste*-li-os
Stilianos	Sti-li-a-*nos*
Vouliagmeni	Vou-li-ag-*me*-ni
Yannopoulos	Yan-*no*-pou-los
Yoakim	Yo-a-*kim*

ACT ONE

Time: the 1950s. A working class neighbourhood in Athens. The play takes place in a courtyard with several one room apartments. A family lives in each one. On the left is the apartment where JORDAN's *family lives. It has a window looking onto the courtyard, and close to the window is a wooden stairway leading up to the terrace. This area is well cared for and pleasant to look at. There are poles with children's windmills nailed to the top of them. There is also a little aeroplane. The few railings, as well as the two flowerpots on the parapet, are painted in gaudy colours. The door of* JORDAN'S *apartment is at the back. It does not open onto the courtyard.*

On the right is ANNETO'S *apartment. This is almost a two-storey building, because above the usual ground floor apartment, there is a fairly big loft, set back, with a fairly large open area in front of it — rather like a balcony without railings.*

Between these two apartments is a broad passageway leading towards the back where the other apartments are.

There are stone steps in front of the apartments belonging to ANNETO *and* JORDAN. *This area serves as a kind of living room for the women. There are a number of stools and packing cases lying around.*

What should characterize the set is the feeling that the area is communal, vibrant and full of life.

The play opens at dusk. It is the end of summer. MARIA *is sitting on a step on the right, embroidering a tablecloth.*

VOULA *has set up a mirror on the wooden stairway, and is cutting her own hair.*

At the window outside JORDAN'S *house, his son* YANNIS *is reading a book.*

JORDAN, *with a bundle of bedding on his shoulder, comes from the back and goes up to the terrace.*

VOULA: Yanni.
YANNIS: Eh?
VOULA: Your father's going up to the observatory.
MARIA: He's right on time. It's sunset after all.
    (YANNIS *doesn't speak.* JORDAN *spreads the bedding on the*

terrace. VOULA *goes over to* MARIA.)
VOULA: Have I left any hairs on my neck?
MARIA: Turn round so I can have a look.
VOULA: Here, take the scissors and cut any you see. (*She gives* MARIA *the scissors and crouches with her back towards* MARIA.)
MARIA: Why did you cut it yourself?
VOULA: If I had the money, I'd go to the hairdresser, but where am I supposed to get any?
MARIA: You had a bundle of it last week.
VOULA: So we had, but *now* we're flat broke.
MARIA: You're both crazy, you know that?
VOULA: Is it my fault? My husband's hands are like sieves, he can't keep a ten drachma piece in them.
MARIA: Yes, but you're the same. I never hear you say no when he's after drinking money.
VOULA: Why should I say no to him? We're young. Shouldn't we enjoy ourselves a bit?
(JORDAN *comes down from the terrace, and goes off to the back.*)
MARIA: You should be putting something aside.
VOULA: Think what you like! If we had regular money coming in, well then, yes. But he works for one week, and then he's idle for the next two!
MARIA: Is there any need to squander it all at once and then go hungry?
VOULA: When you've had a hard time for two weeks, you want to relax. It's natural.
MARIA: Here, take the scissors. I've tidied you up.
VOULA: Thanks, love. Do you want me to cut yours?
MARIA: It doesn't need it.
(ANNETO, *who is sixty years old, comes out of her apartment. She sings while she dusts a canvas suitcase with a hand brush.*)
ANNETO (*sings*): "Romona, I hear the mission bells above, Romona, they're singing out our song of love. I press you, caress you and bless the day you taught me to care. To always remember the rambling rose you wore in your hair."
MARIA (*glances towards* ANNETO): She went to the bank yesterday and sent all her money to England. She's left herself penniless again, the daft old woman.
VOULA: How'll she afford her trip to Paros?
MARIA: Somebody'll pay for it. Either that or she'll lift her pension

ACT ONE

for the whole year.

VOULA (*to* ANNETO): So, you're leaving us tomorrow?

ANNETO (*in mock self-pity*): I'll go away. Then I won't be a nuisance to you anymore.

VOULA: Oh come on, don't start your whinging.

ANNETO: I'm just a lonely old woman with one foot in the grave. I'm annoying you all here, so I'll go away, and leave you in peace.

VOULA: Ah, the poor soul. Give over! We're all neighbours here. There must have been a misunderstanding.

ANNETO (*dismissively*): A misunderstanding. That's all very well. But you're always drumming it into me that I upset you. Is that not so?

MARIA: If we said a word out of place, you would take it personally.

ANNETO: We don't behave like that in England! I'm leaving. I'm going to spend a year in Paros, so you can all relax. And if I never see you again, forgive me, and may God forgive you. (*She pretends to weep.*)

VOULA (*running to her*): Oh come now, stop crying. You know how much we love you!

ANNETO: Do you think I don't love all of you?

MARIA: How could we live without you?

ANNETO: How could *I*?

MARIA (*also coming to* ANNETO): Come, sit down here you whinger. Give me the suitcase and *I'll* dust it for you.

ANNETO: Leave it. You'll dirty your hands. I have dusted it, dear.

VOULA: We'll get your things ready. You just sit and rest.

ANNETO (*completely forgetting her crying fit*): Good. I'll have a cigarette. But I'll fix my own things. I like packing my suitcase. I love it.

VOULA: And take your nice, soft pillow with you.

(ANNETO *sits down and lights a cigarette. The other two sit down as well.*)

ANNETO (*teasingly to* MARIA): Tell me, are you still acting Penelope for us?

MARIA: Who's this Penelope you're talking about?

ANNETO (*laughing*): Then why've you been sewing and unstitching this tablecloth for the last two years?

MARIA: Excuse me, your grace, it isn't a year since I started it.

VOULA (*to* ANNETO): You think she should have it finished by now?

ANNETO: Indeed she should.

MARIA: I'm not working at it all the time, that's why. I work at it when I feel like it. It passes the time for me.

ANNETO: If I were in your place, I'd go for a stroll, to be seen and get a breath of air!

MARIA: Oh, of course.

ANNETO: What do you mean "Oh, of course"? Just because your husband's a stoker, you have to make do with the embroidery? You can be sure that handsome young man is getting on fine whichever port he's in.

VOULA: Are you listening to this?

MARIA: Where would I go out to alone? Where?

ANNETO: It's because you're alone that you ought to go out.

MARIA: What would you know? What are you getting at?

ANNETO: It doesn't take a philosopher to understand.

VOULA: Ah, *now* we're with you.

ANNETO: We know what's on your mind when you work like a madwoman on the embroidery.

MARIA: Give over.

VOULA: She's got to you again? She's got to you?

MARIA: Shut up, both of you. The men'll hear you.

(JORDAN *goes up to the terrace again, carrying a bottle of wine and a dish of fried octopus and such.*)

ANNETO: Have a lovely evening, Mr Jordan.

JORDAN: Come up and join me!

MARIA: Tell me, Mrs Anneto . . .

ANNETO: The dust in that bloody suitcase! In England, we don't have any dust.

MARIA: Tell me, where will you get the money for the journey?

(JORDAN *comes down from the terrace, and goes out to the back.*)

ANNETO: I cashed four pension cheques, and borrowed a bit more. I'll make up the rest with the rent.

VOULA: What rent?

ANNETO: From the apartment, my dear.

MARIA: Which apartment?

ANNETO: This one here, if you please. Have I any other?

MARIA (*to* VOULA): What did I tell you? Didn't I say that she'll go her own way in the end without asking anybody? There you are.

VOULA (*angrily*): She is *not* doing that!

ACT ONE

ANNETO (*bursting out excitedly*): I'll do it all right! It's my room, and I'm subletting it. I'll do what I want. It's my own apartment I'm giving up, not yours. So there!
MARIA: You insensitive... We're like a family here, and you're going to move a strange woman in on us.
VOULA (*to* ANNETO): She's right. How do we know what sort of riff-raff she is?
ANNETO: It isn't a woman. It's a man.
MARIA: A man?
ANNETO: A young man, a delight. And what hair... God forgive me!
VOULA: Since my husband'll be back soon I'll speak my mind now. You should be ashamed of yourself — and you a woman. How can you move a strange man in here with all these women and young girls, eh? Tell me!
MARIA: No man'll set foot in here! Do you hear me? If he does, I'll call the police!
ANNETO: What have the police got to do with it, woman? Am I putting a dangerous animal in the room, or a smuggler? I'm only putting a man in. If you're shy of him, don't let on... and if you get the hots for him, you'll just have to wash more often. Do you hear!
(JORDAN *comes out with an old rifle, and goes up to the terrace again.* YANNIS *follows him, looking upset.*)
YANNIS: Why do you want the rifle?
JORDAN: Mind your own business.
YANNIS: Wine, food and a quiet life aren't good enough for you, are they? You have to shoot the tomcats as well! What have the world's cats ever done to you, eh?
JORDAN: It's none of your business!
YANNIS: Please...
JORDAN (*turning the rifle on him*): Go away.
ANNETO (*shouting*): Asta. Your son. (*To* YANNIS): Get away from there. You might get shot. That's how he took your mother's breast away.
ASTA (*appearing suddenly*): Where did you see him shooting off my breast, eh?
ANNETO: Everybody knows it.
ASTA: Did you see it?
ANNETO: You didn't show me.
ASTA: Then, if you didn't see it, what are you talking about?

13

ANNETO: I know it's true. What else do you expect me to say? Show us and we'll see if it's true or not.

ASTA: Shame on you. (*She goes towards the back.*)

ANNETO: Strange woman. I called her for her son's sake, and she blames me.

DORA (*coming in wearing a flimsy dressing gown*): Has anybody got the right time?

MARIA: Twenty to seven.

VOULA: Your hair's gorgeous! Did you wash it?

DORA: I have to go out.

VOULA: With *him* again? In the sports car?

DORA: Where can you go in the bus, and especially now in the summer?

(YANNIS *stares at* DORA.)

ANNETO: In England, we always travel in our own car.

DORA: Really?

ANNETO: Of course. In my son-in-law's car.

DORA: It must be nice in London.

ANNETO: You'd take London by storm. Lords would be kissing your feet. Look at that beauty. Look at it. A rose in bloom. (*She spits.*) May you be spared the evil eye ... I don't want to bring you bad luck. A rose in bloom. So, what's been happening? When are you getting engaged?

DORA (*annoyed*): Ach, not *that* again. Whenever he wants.

VOULA: Did you get another love letter from the stranger?

DORA: Here it is. (*Laughing, she takes it out of her pocket.*)

VOULA: Bring it here and give us a laugh.

DORA: Just a minute. Ach, where are the children? Where've they all gone?

YANNIS: What do you want?

DORA: To send them to get my white shoes. I left them in to be cleaned. How can I go there in my dressing gown?

YANNIS: I'll go.

DORA: Oh, not you.

YANNIS: What does it matter?

DORA: Well, OK then, thanks very much. (*Giving him money*): Here. It'll be three drachmas.

YANNIS: Don't bother.

DORA: No, I'm not having you paying. It's enough that you're getting them for me.

YANNIS: It's only three drachmas.

ACT ONE

DORA: It isn't fair. The day before yesterday, you paid two drachmas for hair clips. Take it, otherwise I won't let you go. I'll get angry!
YANNIS: All right. (*He goes to leave.*)
VOULA: Take out the letter now for a laugh.
JORDAN (*in a peremptory tone*): Yanni.
YANNIS: What is it?
JORDAN: Come here.
YANNIS: I'm busy. I'll see you when I come back.
JORDAN: Come here. I want to speak to you.
YANNIS: When I come back. Don't you understand?
JORDAN: And I say come here. Don't you understand *me*?
DORA: Go, Yanni. I'm not in such a hurry for the shoes.
   (YANNIS *goes one or two steps up to the terrace.*)
JORDAN: Do you know what wine is?
YANNIS: It's a drink. What are you on about?
JORDAN: Listen. I'll tell you. Man had troubles in head. He said, "What'll I drink to drown them?" Drink water — nothing. Drank milk — nothing. Troubles here. (*He holds his head.*) Went and drank sherbet, salep, cherry cordial, lemonade, sage tea, nothing, nothing, no good. Troubles still in head and get worse. Then came other man, saintly man, very sympathetic. Says: "Water, milk, salep ... when you drink, they go *down*. You must find other drink to go to head!" Do you understand, Yanni?
YANNIS: I understand!
JORDAN: Other man plants vineyard, makes wine, drinks wine. Goes to head! Other, better world. Christ appears. Drinks too. "Bravo," he says. "Bravo", and blesses wine. "This is my blood." That's what wine is. Go now.
ANNETO: I could listen for hours to that man — for hours.
MARIA: You're as mad as he is!
ANNETO (*to* MARIA *and* VOULA): Since when have you understood so much then, you insensitive, impertinent ...
VOULA (*to* ANNETO): Stop it you. (*To* DORA): Where's the letter?
DORA (*opening it*): Here you are. Listen. (*To* YANNIS, *who hesitates*): Do you want to hear it too?
YANNIS: No. How could the poor man know when he was writing it that so many people would hear his secrets?
DORA: He shouldn't write them then.
YANNIS: He wants to tell you he loves you. Is that so funny?

DORA: *I* find it funny.

YANNIS: If I could make you understand how badly you're behaving. (*He goes out.*)

VOULA: Come on. Read it for a laugh.

(*Miaowing can be heard from the adjoining roof.* JORDAN *grabs his rifle and shoots. The miaowing stops.*)

DORA (*reading*): "My darling. I wish I had the strength of mind not to write to you again, but I haven't. All day yesterday when I managed not to grab pen and paper, I felt as if my tongue had been cut out, as if I'd lost my voice. I believe that whatever I have to say as a human being, I must say to you. The dreams I have about my life, about what I want to become, everything I dream of I imagine with you beside me, belonging to me, close to me."

(ANNETO *listens, deeply moved; almost ecstatic. Similarly* MARIA, *who has paused in her embroidery.*)

VOULA: Ah, the poor man!

ANNETO: Shhh!

DORA: "I know very well that you're not happy with what you're doing. I know that the man with the short jacket and sports car who comes to take you away every evening from our neighbourhood is not the one you want. I've seen you many times coming back at night, tired and sad. You often come back with tears in your eyes, and murmuring to yourself as if you were talking in your sleep."

(ANNETO *weeps.*)

MARIA: Read on.

DORA: He's making it all up. I've never cried, and I've never talked to myself.

ANNETO: It doesn't matter. Finish it!

DORA: "On such nights, I long to reveal myself to you, and tell you . . ."

BABIS (*coming in shouting and bustling, laden with parcels*): Voulaaa!

VOULA: Here I am.

BABIS: Get dressed.

VOULA: Where are we going?

BABIS: Wherever you like. Where do you fancy . . . the sea, the mountains, the plains? You decide.

VOULA: Really?

BABIS: Come and give me a hand. Can't you see I'm carrying a

ACT ONE

cartload of parcels like a porter? Are you blind?
VOULA: What are they?
BABIS: How would I know? Meat, fish, cheese, salami, sardines, fruit, chocolate. I hardly know what they are.
VOULA (*with great pleasure*): *You* didn't buy them then?
BABIS: Do I care what I bought? What would *I* know about shopping? I said to him: "Give me some of everything."
VOULA (*very pleased*): What'll we do with so many things?
BABIS: Stop it, will you! Are we going to talk about food now? Let it be. It won't be wasted.
VOULA (*unloading the parcels from* BABIS): He gave you the money ... the one who ...
BABIS: You're a funny one, you know that? All right, I know we're all friends here — Maria, Dora and Anneto. But do you think I can shout about the whys and wherefores? Can I?
ANNETO: Of course not.
BABIS: Don't misunderstand me now. I'm not showing off. But that's the way it is.
ANNETO: So it is.
VOULA (*kissing him noisily*): Sweetie pie.
BABIS (*wiping his cheek*): Don't be disgusting. Here, take this. (VOULA. *who is on her way to their apartment stops short.* BABIS *takes a necklace ostentatiously out of his pocket.*)
VOULA: What's this?
BABIS: Do you like it?
VOULA: Where did you find it?
BABIS: Stop that! (*He puts it into his pocket indignantly.*) To hell with it! I'll throw it away.
VOULA: Sweetie.
BABIS: Everybody's listening to you. What do you mean where did I find it? I forked out good money for it.
VOULA: Seriously?
BABIS: Here, take it. (*He puts it round her neck.*) How does that look to you, Dora? It's nice, isn't it? You, Maria, what do you think? It suits her, eh? Doesn't it suit her?
ANNETO: Ah, it's beautiful, child. May you have health to wear it.
DORA: It's very chic.
VOULA: Thanks.
BABIS: It's chic, eh. It is, isn't it?
MARIA: It suits her.
BABIS: Of course it does. Just look how it suits her.

THE COURTYARD OF WONDERS

(VOULA *is proud and very moved.*)
BABIS: It suits her *very* well. (*He laughs happily. He nips* VOULA *on the bottom.*)
(*Cackling,* VOULA *gathers up the parcels to take them inside.*)
MARIA: Voula, tell them about the tenant that the old woman is bringing in.
VOULA: Not now!
ANNETO: It's wonderful dear, wonderful. Health to wear it, dear. Health to wear it.
VOULA: Thanks. Thanks. (*She takes the parcels and goes inside.*)
MARIA: She nearly came to blows with the old woman about the tenant, and now she's forgotten it.
BABIS: Well then, what do you think, Dora? If Voula dressed herself up, she could show them, eh?
DORA: She's attractive all right.
BABIS: Yes, the hussy . . . she *is* attractive.
MARIA: Babi, have you heard? The old woman has sublet her apartment. She's moving a stranger in on us. You're a man. Have a word with her. Scare her.
BABIS: All right. I'll speak to her. Dora, I've put some money aside to buy her a frock on the quiet — for a surprise, as they say — a surprise.
DORA: I understand.
BABIS: Being a man, I don't know anything about it. When it comes to men's clothes, I have taste, I assure you, excellent taste. But with women's clothes . . . will you come with me tomorrow or the day after and choose? You'd know what to get.
DORA: Whenever you want.
BABIS: Not a word, eh? It's a surprise, right?
MARIA: Babi, speak to Anneto. We're all women here. How can she bring in a bachelor, a stranger?
BABIS: All right, agreed. I'll speak to her.
(BABIS *goes off to his apartment. As he approaches* ANNETO, *who has been humming, she smiles at him.*)
ANNETO: May she have health to wear it, the poor thing, health to wear it. It's beautiful.
BABIS: I like the fine things in life.
ANNETO: You're a gentleman.
BABIS (*scratches his neck, and laughs with pleasure.*): I'm a bastard, I am. (*He goes out.*)
ANNETO: For three days, he left her with nothing to eat. Yesterday,

ACT ONE

he gave her a beating. Today, he buys her jewellery. Good God! (JORDAN *has been on the lookout again, and shoots the rifle towards the roofs. Terrified miaowings and clatter.*)

DORA (*startled*): You gave me a fright.

JORDAN (*sees* DORA, *gazes at her, puts his hand to his mouth and sings with enthusiasm the Greek urban blues refrain*): "Amaaaaan Amaaaaan".

(ASTA *comes into the courtyard carrying a slice of bread and shouting "Yoakim". She stops suddenly as if she felt a severe chest pain. She leans against something, so as not to fall.* DORA *and* MARIA *run to her. On the terrace,* JORDAN *continues singing.* ANNETO *goes into her room.*)

DORA (*to* ASTA): What's the matter?

ASTA: The usual.

MARIA: Is it your heart again?

ASTA: The old washtub's worn out. It has a hole in it. It doesn't work well anymore. That blessed child out playing again! He didn't come home at lunch time for a bite to eat.

MARIA: Sit down here.

ASTA: It's nothing. It's gone now. (*She looks as if she is still in pain, but moves limping towards the street calling for Yoakim.*)

DORA: Mr Jordan, your wife isn't well.

JORDAN: You should have seen her in her youth.

DORA: I'm sure, but now she's ill.

JORDAN: In her youth. The sun in her hair, the sky in her eyes!

DORA: Now what's he going to do? He'll drop dead.

JORDAN: She's changed. She's cha . . . (*He lies down on his back on the blankets.*)

(YANNIS *comes in carrying the high-heeled shoes.* ANNETO *comes out of her apartment carrying a tray with Greek coffees.*)

ANNETO (*calling out*): Babi. Voula. I'm bringing you a coffee. Open up.

VOULA (*from inside*): Come on in. We have some cakes.

(ANNETO *goes into their apartment.*)

MARIA: We're all friends again. God bless us.

DORA: What do *you* care?

MARIA: That a strange man'll be in here. Day and night.

YANNIS: Sorry I'm a bit late. He hadn't varnished the soles.

DORA: Thank you *very* much.

YANNIS: Haven't you got small feet.

DORA: Do you think so?

YANNIS: To fit into these tiny shoes. When I was holding them, it seemed to me as if . . .
DORA: What time is it?
YANNIS: Seven!
DORA: I must get dressed. Thank you.
YANNIS (*ironically*): Wonderful.
   (DORA *goes out.* YANNIS *gazes after her.* MARIA *finds the stranger's letter beside her where she had forgotten it, and puts it hastily into her pocket. Outside,* ASTA *can be heard calling: "Yoakim. Your bread, son." A sturdy, thirty-five year old man comes in. His name is Stratos. He glances round the courtyard, and at* YANNIS *and* MARIA.)
STRATOS (*in a purposeful tone*): A Mrs Anneto lives here?
MARIA (*paying particular attention to him*): Yes, she lives here.
STRATOS: Thanks. (*He looks around the courtyard again.*) Where is she? Is she out?
MARIA (*to* YANNIS): Yanni, she's at Voula's.
YANNIS: I'll call her. (*He goes to the back.*)
   (MARIA *stays silent, while embroidering nervously.* STRATOS *looks at her sideways as if he were sizing her up.* MARIA, *as if she can't stand any more of it, gathers up her things and leaves.* STRATOS *gazes after her. Outside,* ASTA *can still be heard calling "Yoakim".* JORDAN *raises himself up, and looks at the stranger.*)
JORDAN: Evening.
STRATOS: Good evening.
JORDAN: Sit down.
STRATOS (*sits on a chair*): Do you live up there?
JORDAN: On summer evenings, I live here.
STRATOS: You're well off up there.
JORDAN: I drink my wine. I remember things. I see sky and sleep. I can't be down there anymore. My heart's weary.
STRATOS: You're not far wrong. But you should put an awning over you.
JORDAN: Over me?
STRATOS: Sometimes it rains a bit at night.
JORDAN: Good rain. When it rains, I open my mouth and drink it all. Roof never . . . never. Sky better roof. Three times they took roof from me — three times. (*Making a sound like someone chasing a dog away*): Ouf! Nobody take sky from me. Ouf!
STRATOS: You're right there!

ACT ONE

JORDAN: Have you good job?
STRATOS: Plumber.
JORDAN: Plumbers good men. Tiring work?
STRATOS: It can get tiring.
JORDAN: Everybody tired, good people. I work at furnace.
STRATOS: In a foundry?
JORDAN: No, roof tiles.
STRATOS: Do they pay well?
JORDAN: Listen. Thousands of roofs have been made with my sweat. I haven't my own roof over my own head. What do you think, my friend? Give me your opinion. Do they pay well?
STRATOS: That's the way it goes!
JORDAN (*raising himself slightly*): I'll get a glass and give you some wine.
STRATOS: Don't bother yourself.
JORDAN: I don't mind. A pleasure that you drink with me.
STRATOS: I don't want a drink.
JORDAN: Why not?
STRATOS: You drink it.
(JORDAN, *annoyed, lies down on his bedding.* ANNETO *comes in with* YANNIS *behind her.*)
ANNETO: The man himself.
STRATOS: Good evening.
ANNETO: I was expecting you.
STRATOS: Which apartment is it?
ANNETO: Come and see it.
STRATOS: Is it over there?
ANNETO: Yes, here.
STRATOS: It's rather different from what you told me.
ANNETO: How "rather different", young man?
STRATOS: You said it had a door onto the street.
ANNETO: And hasn't it?
STRATOS: This is a courtyard. It isn't a street.
ANNETO: And how far is it from the street? A couple of steps.
STRATOS: Missus, I told you that if it was inside a courtyard, it wouldn't suit me.
ANNETO: Why? Are people who live in courtyards not human beings? In England, we always live in courtyards.
STRATOS: I'm sure you do, but I don't like forty pairs of eyes looking at me going in and out.
ANNETO: Don't worry about that. Everybody here minds their own

THE COURTYARD OF WONDERS

business ... not that they don't know their neighbours, you understand.

STRATOS: You talk too much.

(OLGA *comes in. She is a young woman with a certain warmth in her face, and in her bearing. Nevertheless, her look and her expression indicate a reserved character.*)

OLGA: Good evening.

YANNIS & ANNETO: Good evening Olya.

(OLGA *moves on, and goes off to the back.*)

STRATOS: What did you call her? Olya?

ANNETO: Olya. She's Russian. Her real name is Olga, but we call her Olya. She lives with us, but she doesn't get on well with her husband. Don't you think she's attractive?

STRATOS (*making a move to leave*): Goodnight.

ANNETO: At least have a look inside. The walls are papered like in England. Look at it first, and if it doesn't suit you ...

(STRATOS *stops.*)

ANNETO: Wait a minute — I'll tidy up some rubbish inside. (*She goes into her apartment.*)

STRATOS (*to* JORDAN): You're well off up there. (*To* YANNIS): Tell me, is this woman here English?

YANNIS: Her daughter married an Englishman.

STRATOS: Did the old woman live in England before that?

YANNIS: Not at all. Last year she went for two months.

BABIS (*coming hurriedly from the back, dressed in a suit.*): Come on pet, move yourself.

VOULA (*shouting from inside*): I'm coming.

BABIS (*sees something outside, and runs shouting*): Taxi! Stop! Taxi! Come over here and wait. (*Calling towards the back*): Come on love. The taxi's waiting. (*He whistles happily.*)

YANNIS: Have a good time.

BABIS: How are things, Yanni? How're we getting on?

(VOULA *comes hastily into the courtyard, singing to herself. She is also dressed in her best clothes.* BABIS *takes her arm, and, singing the same tune to himself now, they go out.* ASTA *comes in, still holding the piece of bread. She speaks to* STRATOS *as if she had known him for years.*)

ASTA: She nearly fainted yesterday with the beating he gave her. Now he's taking her out in a taxi. And I haven't found Yoakim. He didn't have a bite to eat the whole afternoon — not a bite. They go to the building site up there, and play with the bricks.

ACT ONE

(*To* YANNIS): Are *you* here? Do you want some bread and sugar?
YANNIS: I'm not hungry.
ASTA: Why don't you go to the square?
YANNIS: What for?
ASTA: You could do with a little exercise.
YANNIS: Walk up and down annoying the girls, you mean!
ASTA: Well go to the café, then!
YANNIS: I don't want to. I don't like it.
ASTA: Your friends'll be there. Go on. I can't look at you huddled up silent in here.
YANNIS: I can't stand the café.
ASTA: Why don't you go to the cinema?
YANNIS: You want me to fork out five drachmas every day for the cinema?
ASTA: Climb up the tree and see the film. Everybody watches it from there.
YANNIS: *All right.* I'll go for a stroll.
ASTA (*to* JORDAN): Do you want some bread and sugar? Don't stay up there with only your vest on. You'll catch cold. There's a breeze.
(JORDAN *doesn't pay any attention to her.* ASTA *goes to the back.* ANNETO *comes out of her apartment.*)
ANNETO: Come in, Mr Strato, come in. Facing us, we have Mount Hymettus. The sun wakes us every morning. It comes out from there. The apartment's in a very nice position. From the terrace, not this one, the one next to it, you can see Athens spread out in front of you, as far as Faliron. And the American navy has arrived. You can see their ships in the harbour. Come in.
(STRATOS *follows her into her apartment.* MARIA *and* OLGA *appear from the back.*)
MARIA: They've gone in to let him see it.
OLGA: I know, but what can *I* do?
MARIA: Tell your husband. *I* haven't got a husband! If he were here, he'd deal with it! Will *you* feel safe enough to come and go as you please? Will *you* be able to sleep with the windows open, sit on the stairway in your nightdress, clean yourself up in the washroom stark naked — tell me, will you? Will you be able to do all this with a strange man around?
OLGA: When my husband comes, I'll tell him.
MARIA: When'll he be back?
OLGA: He'll be late this evening.

YANNIS: He's at the café.
OLGA: He can't be. He told me that . . .
MARIA (*nodding towards* YANNIS): Let *him* go and call him. Yanni, will you?
OLGA (*quite angrily*): Go where? I told you, he's not in the café.
MARIA: Well, Yannis saw him.
OLGA: He must've been mistaken.
MARIA: He saw him. Didn't you say so?
YANNIS: I . . . I'm not sure.
OLGA: It's impossible. He had to look for a job today. He'll be finished late. And besides, he doesn't set foot in the café anymore. He swore to me that he won't play cards ever again.
(STELIOS, OLGA's *husband, comes in.*)
STELIOS: Good evening.
MARIA: We were just talking about you. We were looking for you.
STELIOS (*to* OLGA): I've finished early as you see. The heat. (*He wipes away the sweat.*)
MARIA: Stelio, you've come at the right time.
STELIOS: What's happening?
MARIA: The old woman is bringing in a tenant.
STELIOS: What kind of tenant?
MARIA: Whatever kind he is, hadn't we agreed that she mustn't move a stranger in on us?
STELIOS: Don't worry. I'll settle it!
MARIA: She's already done it. He's inside!
STELIOS: Don't fret yourself. I'll take care of this.
MARIA: We agreed not to let her upset us again, but Voula and Babis don't care.
STELIOS: At least *I* care as far as this is concerned! If necessary, I'll get tough with her. What's been happening, Olga? Where did you go?
OLGA: To my aunt's. Tell me, how did the job hunting go?
STELIOS: I'll tell you later. I'll tell you inside, where we'll have peace. We have to see how things are going to turn out with this little old woman.
OLGA: When'll you tell me? I can't wait!
STELIOS: Leave me alone, will you. Do you know what I think? The old woman's tenant can go to hell!
MARIA: We're lucky to have a man like you here.
STELIOS: I will not allow us to be treated like this!
(*At this moment, voices are heard outside. "He came in here. I*

ACT ONE

saw him." A man comes in angrily, and speaks to STELIOS.)
MAN: Oh, you're here, are you? Cough it up! The twenty drachmas . . . now!
STELIOS (*trying to stay calm*): Are you speaking to me?
MAN: Of course I'm speaking to you. Come on, cough up the twenty drachmas.
STELIOS: First of all, I'd advise you to watch your tongue.
MAN: All right. Would you give me the twenty drachmas now?
OLGA: What twenty drachmas? Who is this?
STELIOS: We're not going to discuss this in my home.
MAN (*grabbing* STELIOS *by the collar, and pulling him*): You want to go outside? Outside then!
STELIOS: Get your hands off me!
MAN: Give me the twenty drachmas. Do you hear? Give them to me!
STELIOS: Don't you lay a finger on me!
OLGA: What's this about? Stelio, what's going on?
MAN: He's a thief. We found three cards under the table, an ace and two queens.
STELIOS: He's a liar, Olga!
MAN: Are you going to give me the twenty drachmas, or aren't you?
(OLGA *covers her face in despair and shame.*)
MARIA: Holy Mother.
STELIOS: Let me go!
MARIA: Leave the man alone. Olga!
MAN: No I won't! Give me my twenty drachmas.
STELIOS: What twenty drachmas? What have I got to do with your twenty drachmas?
MAN: What else can I say to him? I'll smash your teeth in, you thieving little shit! Give me the twenty drachmas.
YANNIS: Put the man down.
STELIOS: Call the police.
MAN: Never mind the police, you thieving little bastard.
STELIOS: Let me go! Let me go!
MAN: No, I won't let you go. Give me the twenty drachmas!
STELIOS: Yanni, call the police.
MAN (*dragging* STELIOS *along*): *I'll* bring you to the police.
MARIA: Help! Help!
STELIOS: Let me go!
MAN: The twenty drachmas. The twenty drachmas. You're all scum!

(ANNETO *and* STRATOS *come out.* OLGA's *whole body is trembling.*)

STELIOS: Let go of me, you bastard!

MAN (*gives* STELIOS *a heavy blow that lays him out on the ground*): Bastard, eh?

STELIOS: I'll sue you.

OLGA (*enraged*): Get up! Hit him!

STELIOS: I'll sue him!

OLGA: Hit him back!

STELIOS: You're my witness. I'll sue him.

OLGA (*hysterically*): No, I want you to hit him! Hit him ... kill him!

STELIOS: Olga!

OLGA: Hit him! Hit him!

STELIOS: *I'm* a ... Olga ... I'll get the law onto him.

OLGA: Hit him!

STELIOS: *I'm* a gentleman. I don't ...

OLGA: Hit him!

STELIOS: Olga ...

OLGA: No, no, no. *You* hit him!

(STRATOS *stands face to face with the man, and gives him a blow that sends him almost outside.*)

MAN (*going away shouting*): Thieves! Swindlers! Scum!

(OLGA *gazes at* STRATOS.)

STELIOS (*getting up from the ground, and glaring at* STRATOS): Who told you to ... (*He goes off towards the back.*)

(OLGA *bursts into tears.*)

MARIA: Let's go in. Come on.

(*She takes* OLGA *around the waist, and almost drags her towards her apartment.*)

ANNETO: He'll have started playing cards again. And when *he* starts ...

YANNIS: If I could make him understand how badly he's behaving.

ANNETO (*to* STRATOS): Your hand's bleeding. Come and I'll put some disinfectant on it.

STRATOS: Don't bother.

ANNETO: They've interrupted us ... just when we were about to reach an agreement. Come inside.

STRATOS (*following her reluctantly, and passing* JORDAN, *who hasn't stirred throughout the previous quarrel*): Man, you've found yourself a good berth up there. (*He goes into the*

ACT ONE

apartment with ANNETO.)

DORA (*coming into the courtyard, dressed to go out.*): What time is it? Have you the right time?

YANNIS: Twenty past seven.

DORA: I've lost that letter. Did you come across it by any chance?

YANNIS: You've lost it?

DORA: Yes, I remember folding it about this big. Don't worry. Forget it. He'll send another one. Bye.

YANNIS: Where could it have fallen?

DORA: We were sitting here. Don't worry about it. (*She goes out.*) (YANNIS *looks around for the letter. He strikes a match to get some light.* JORDAN *sits up and looks into the yard.*)

JORDAN: Yanni.

YANNIS: What do you want?

JORDAN: Come and I'll tell you.

YANNIS: Again?

JORDAN: Come here, Yanni. I can talk only to you. You have good heart — like flowering garden.

YANNIS (*approaching the bed*): I'm listening.

JORDAN: Yanni.

YANNIS: Yes.

JORDAN: What are stars?

YANNIS: Planets.

JORDAN: Eh?

YANNIS: Planets.

JORDAN (*makes a face, and a gesture of disgust*): Listen. *I'll* tell you. God said: "There must be night. Poor people lie down, rest, close their eyes." He sends sun away. Takes black sheet of paper. Covers sky. Looks from below. "Not good," he says. "Pitch black." Takes pin and — tsik tsik — makes little hole here, there — makes thousands. Sun shines from inside. Stars come out. Man see. Man is pleased. God also says: "Must lie down, rest, close his eyes. In his mind stars become good dreams." (*He lies down again on his back.*)

(YANNIS *walks over to the middle of the yard. He lights another match, and searches again for the letter.*)

LIGHTS OUT

ACT TWO

Two months later, on a Sunday morning. JORDAN *is repairing his terrace.* STRATOS *is sitting nonchalantly on the stairway of* ANNETO's *house strumming a guitar. His shirt is open, revealing a gold cross around his neck.* STELIOS *is beside him. A short distance away from them,* DORA *is tanning her legs in the sun, and reading the magazine "Treasure".*

STELIOS: He's been fixing it, mending it and decorating it for years now. And what is it but an old bit of a terrace. Isn't man wonderful? (*To* STRATOS): Have you ever been to the races?

STRATOS: Do you take me for a fool?

STELIOS: Oh, come now — don't be so negative. It all depends on forecasting. For example, I bet that if they buried Jordan on the terrace when he dies, his soul would get away more easily. So, you could say that a horse race is also a question of forecasting. You have your information. You're a winner. If you haven't, you're like a lamb to the slaughter.

STRATOS: You talk too much.

STELIOS: I'm just explaining to you.

JORDAN: Yannis, where is Yannis?

STELIOS: Jordan's the first Pharaoh I've known personally. The Pharaohs of Egypt — you've heard of them — they prepared their tombs when they were young, and they were free from worries. It's the same with Jordan. You see, we have pyramids in Athens too. We have everything. Last Sunday, Malamatas, the barber, went to the races with a hundred drachmas, and came back with three and a half thousand. *I* told him who to back.

STRATOS: Good for you.

STELIOS: I see you haven't one grey hair on your head. Mine's full of them. I'm getting old. Dora knew the shop. She used to come to it.

STRATOS: What shop?

STELIOS: The second one. You're too young to have seen the first one. The Occupation did for it. You were a child then. I'm talking about the second one. It might have been just a door in Athena Street, but there was a time when I had two hundred thousand worth of goods in there. Isn't that so, Dora? Tourism

ACT TWO

killed that one off. They had to clean up the main streets.

DORA: You're casting a shadow. Get out of the sun.

STELIOS: Why don't you go for a swim today? You always go on a Sunday.

DORA: The carburettor's broken. The car's at the garage.

STELIOS: When are you getting engaged?

DORA: Are you all still on at that?

STELIOS: It's the first time I've asked. Has he money, Dora? A lot of money?

DORA: So it seems.

STELIOS: And to think he got it making those cigarette holders.

DORA: There's a whole factory. He doesn't make them himself.

STELIOS: That's it. You have to have capital. I have first class ideas, but I haven't got capital. In the third race, Asnapour and Misiri will bring in eight hundred drachmas. That's a world class pair, you'll see. Misiri, Asian and Chrisoula together could get four or five thousand.

BABIS (*coming from the back swearing*): To hell with women. Ungrateful bitches.

DORA: What's wrong with you two *now*?

BABIS: We're divorcing.

DORA: Again?

BABIS: It's over.

STRATOS: Come on, Babi. Control yourself.

BABIS: I'm divorcing her. I'm leaving.

DORA: Why?

BABIS: What kind of a woman is she? Tell me, Dora. What kind? Any other man would have killed her!

STRATOS: The day before yesterday you were fine!

BABIS: Don't ever get involved with them. You hear me? Don't ever get married, my friend. You'll be done for.

VOULA (*comes out and leaves a small suitcase at her husband's feet*): I've put your underwear in here.

BABIS: Bring the other clothes! All of them!

VOULA: You'll just have to wait.

STELIOS (*to them both*): Listen . . .

VOULA: Speak to *him* — the Neanderthal.

BABIS: You've been going on at me since early this morning — and on a Sunday too.

DORA: Voula. Voula. Voula. Listen to me. (*She runs after* VOULA, *who goes off to the back.*)

29

JORDAN: Yannis — hey there, where is Yannis?
BABIS: I'll go. It'll be for my own good.
STELIOS: Where are you running off to? Sit down and we'll ... we're like a family here.
BABIS: I'll get the forms. I'll go to Australia.
STELIOS: Can one just go?
BABIS: Why not?
STELIOS: It'll be two or three years before your turn comes up.
BABIS: With fifteen hundred drachmas, you can be there in two months. I know somebody who can arrange it.
STELIOS: With only fifteen hundred? More like seven and a half thousand — well, more or less.
BABIS: All right, and another few thousand for the fare ... say twelve thousand.
STELIOS: Is that all? And you're fixed up forever ... for your whole life?
BABIS: There's work there. Real work. As long as you've got hands, you can work. And if you're able enough, you can set up a nice little business of your own. That's the way it works over there. You can do well for yourself.
STELIOS: I'm sure. The soil is virgin. It wants men. It supports them so well, that they don't ever want to leave. It's not driving them away all the time.
BABIS: They even find gold. There are wild places where man has never set foot. They find gold and oil. Just like in the films.
STELIOS: All that for only twelve thousand ...
(VOULA *hurries in again, carrying a bundle. She puts it down beside the suitcase.* DORA *is coming behind her.*)
VOULA: Here's the rest. Goodbye!
DORA: Have you both gone mad?
VOULA: Let him go and leave me in peace.
BABIS: No. I'll stay so's you can nag me to death.
VOULA: You should be ashamed of yourself for leaving me without a drachma for three days.
BABIS: Me? (*He snorts in anger.*) Rubbish. Do you know any other woman who behaves like you? Do you? Whenever I haven't a drachma, you despise me, ignore me, treat me like dirt. Do you know any other woman who would do that?
VOULA: *I* do that? God forgive you for telling such lies, you ungrateful ...
BABIS: Lies, are they?

ACT TWO

VOULA: When you haven't any money, you come in with a big, long face, all perverse and quarrelsome. And me, your poor wife, says, "What does it matter?" and kisses you and fusses over you.
BABIS: So *I'm* the stubborn one?
VOULA: Did I ever complain when we hadn't anything to eat?
BABIS: You've such a face on you!
VOULA: You behave like a barbarian. When you've no money, you're a swine.
BABIS: Right, that's it! (*Lifting the suitcase and the bundle to leave*): We can both start over again. We're still young.
STRATOS: Don't be hasty, man. Don't be hasty.
MARIA (*hurrying in looking pleased*): There's a letter from Mrs Anneto.
STELIOS: What do you know! She's remembered us at last.
DORA: What does she say to you?
MARIA: It's for all of us. Listen.
STELIOS: For all of us? Read it then.
MARIA: "My dear children — Maria, Olga, Dora, Voula, Stelio, Babi and you, Strato . . ."
DORA: The poor soul. She calls us her children.
STELIOS: She's a fine woman!
MARIA: "I'm well, thank God, as I hope the rest of you are. I'm having a nice time here in the village. Everybody was pleased to see me — relatives, friends and acquaintances. You can't imagine how well they've been looking after me. I've so many friends that they come along two at a time, and invite me to eat with them. I've gone on trips, and to a couple of fairs, and lit a candle for each of you."
VOULA: The poor soul. God bless her.
JORDAN: That Yannis has got lost today.
MARIA: "I think of you every day, especially in the evening when we'd sit in our courtyard and eat together and chat. We were always friendly and loving, like a family. Next week, I'll send you a basket of fruit and some cheese to share out among you."
BABIS: We'll certainly drink to the health of Mrs Anneto.
MARIA: "Greetings to Jordan, Asta, and little Yannis. I kiss you all, my children. Until we meet again next year. Anneto." The soul.
STELIOS: A wonderful person. A big heart.
MARIA: I said we'd get a letter from her. I dreamt about her.
VOULA: And she's sending us fruit and cheese, the soul.

BABIS: I hope you enjoy it. *I'll* not be here. (*He makes a move to go.*)
DORA: Babi, don't do this.
MARIA: Are they divorcing again?
STELIOS: Come here, Babi.
VOULA: Let him go. Let him go. He'll be sorry.
DORA: How can you leave her all alone, eh? How can you leave her?
STELIOS: Come back here. (*He runs and catches him.*)
MARIA: Think for a minute about what you're doing.
BABIS: Did she ever think about me? Ever?
STELIOS: What you're doing is a disgrace, Babi.
BABIS: I'm not a villain. Watch what you're saying, or *you'll* get it.
STELIOS: You're a coward, Mr Babi. Where's your self-respect?
BABIS: Don't you tell *me* about bravery and self-respect. Let a man come and tell me, not a pipsqueak like you.
STELIOS: You're breaking up a home, that's all I'm saying. And I'll ignore what you just said.
BABIS: Sort out your own home first, you idiot, you sponger. And then you can sort out mine! If anybody meddles in my business again, I'll punch his lights out!
(*In the meantime, a man has come into the middle of the courtyard holding a tape measure. He places the end of it on the ground.*)
SURVEYOR A (*shouting*): Nine plus sixty. (*He makes a note of the measurement.*)
(*Now everyone becomes aware of him.*)
SURVEYOR A (*speaking hurriedly*): Good day. (*Turning to someone outside*): Come and take it from this point. (*Walking past the tenants, and going towards the back*): Excuse me.
(SURVEYOR B *comes in holding the other end of the tape.*)
SURVEYOR B: Where's the centre?
SURVEYOR A: I've made a line.
SURVEYOR B (*to the tenants*): Move back a bit. Can't you see you're stepping on the tape?
ASTA (*stepping aside in fright*): Ah!
STELIOS: Excuse me. What's this about?
SURVEYOR A (*shouting*): Ten plus twelve. The site has been sold.
MARIA: What site?
SURVEYOR A (*to* SURVEYOR B): Go over there and we'll measure the width. (*To* MARIA): The site has been sold. Somebody else

ACT TWO

has bought it.
VOULA: Are you saying that . . .
STELIOS: So, he's sold it?
MARIA: Who do we deal with now?
SURVEYOR A: And the same here. Sixteen plus seventy.
STELIOS: Who's bought it? Do you know?
SURVEYOR A (*noticing* JORDAN): You, what are you doing there? Oh, you're doing repairs, I see. Better leave it. It's not worth the trouble. Life's too short.
JORDAN: You, come here. I speak you.
SURVEYOR A: Me?
JORDAN: You. Come here.
SURVEYOR A: I can hear you from where I am.
JORDAN: I want *here*.
SURVEYOR A: Oh, all right then. I'll humour you. (*He approaches.*)
JORDAN: Name?
SURVEYOR A: Christos.
JORDAN: Listen. This world. Do you know what it is?
SURVEYOR A: No. *You* tell me.
JORDAN: I'll tell you. God make other world, good world on moon. Have you seen moon with gardens, orchards, pears as big as babies? He made beautiful villages, neat as new five drachma pieces. And lutes, women, food, drink — all for nothing. "Eat, drink, Christian. It's all yours. Be happy, my friends. I'll produce more things," says God. But people treacherous, thieving, dishonest. "All right," says God, cunning. Makes other world, not perfect, famished, food dear. Understand? He made this world. Whoever useless in good world, God seizes his soul by the foot, and sends him spinning like top down to hell. That's what *this* world is!
SURVEYOR A (*to the others*): Who *is* this? He's a laugh. (*Shouting to* SURVEYOR B): All right. Sixteen plus seventy. (*He makes a note.*) Tell me, has that block of flats down there just been built?
STELIOS: Yes, this year.
SURVEYOR A (*he gathers up his tape, and turns to* SURVEYOR B): Have a look at the walls. Are they brick or stone? See if any of those roofs are concrete. (*To the others*): How many families live here?
(ASTA *inadvertently sits on a step on top of the notebook that* SURVEYOR A *has left there.*)
MARIA: Five.

SURVEYOR A: Two of them have been living here since before 1950, I understand?
STELIOS: Two of them, yes. (*Pointing to* MARIA): The lady here, and another one who's away at the moment.
SURVEYOR A: The one who has just sublet her apartment, I believe.
STELIOS: Yes.
SURVEYOR A: She did the right thing.
SURVEYOR B (*approaching*): Most of them are brick. Only one has a flat roof.
SURVEYOR A (*to* ASTA): Get up please, lady. Have you sat on my book?
(ASTA *gets up, looking scared.* SURVEYOR A *picks up the book.*)
SURVEYOR A (*to* SURVEYOR B): Let's go. (*To the others*): Good day to you.
SURVEYOR B (*tonelessly*): Good day.
SURVEYOR A (*leaving with* SURVEYOR B, *and looking at his notebook*): We have, let's say, nine plus sixty and five plus eighty, by ten plus seventy minus thirty plus thirty.
(SURVEYOR A *and* SURVEYOR B *go out.*)
MARIA: They've pulled the rug from under us.
ASTA: Why?
MARIA: Do you think they'll throw us out? To build a new block of flats?
STELIOS: Whatever will be will be. If they throw us out, they throw us out. It won't be the first time, will it?
ASTA: Mr Stelio.
BABIS: What do I care? *I'm* leaving. (*He lifts his suitcase and bundle, and goes off.*)
MARIA: Babi.
STELIOS: Let him go.
MARIA: I'll go and bring him back. How can he leave? He *can't* leave. He's her husband.
STELIOS: He's *her* husband, what does it matter to you?
(VOULA *begins to cry nervously, and runs to the back.*)
DORA: Let them do what they want. (*Sighs with relief, and lies down again to sunbathe.*)
STELIOS: Huh, did you hear what I had to listen to? He called me a pipsqueak and a sponger. We're rid of him anyway, the chancer.
(*A short silence.* STRATOS *strums his guitar again.*)
MARIA (*to* STRATOS): Will you stop twanging that bloody thing ... brrimm, brrimm the whole day!

ACT TWO

DORA: Why? He plays well!
MARIA: I'm not saying he doesn't play well, but can you put up with his passionate songs all day long?
DORA: It's a beautiful tune. It carries you away.
MARIA (*going over to* DORA): Are you going out tonight?
DORA: I am!
MARIA: Where's he taking you?
DORA: I don't know.
MARIA: Do the two of you go out together all the time?
DORA: Most of the time.
STELIOS: When I was younger, music would make me want to dance. It makes me feel so good.
MARIA (*going over towards* STRATOS *who has stopped playing the guitar*): Why aren't you playing anymore?
STRATOS: You told me to stop.
MARIA: Don't let *me* stop you. Are you going to listen to what *I* say? How shiny your hair is.
STRATOS: Brylcreem.
MARIA: No, it's natural. Chestnut hair shines like that.
DORA: And he has some muscles.
STELIOS: It's from hard work. All plumbers are built like that.
MARIA: I wouldn't like to be your wife. I'd be squashed by them.
STRATOS: You reckon?
MARIA: And your shoulders like mountains, and you all hairy. (*She laughs nervously.*) You're disgusting, disgusting. (*She moves away laughing, and goes to the back.*)
STELIOS (*looking out to the street*): Is that Apostolos? No, it'll be Stavros. He's going to the café. (*He goes back over to the others.*) Thank God there's the café on Sunday mornings. Do you go at all?
STRATOS: No!
STELIOS: A hive of activity! Bridge here, poker there, backgammon and piquet. You can hardly get a table to play at. They set themselves up there from nine o'clock. They hear the church service on the radio.
DORA: Shame on them!
STELIOS: Yes, shame on them. (*He stretches out his hand, and holds the cross that* STRATOS *is wearing*): Beautiful cross. Is it gold?
STRATOS: Eighteen carat.
STELIOS: Good Lord, with only twelve thousand drachmas, the

whole of Australia would be in your hand. Here — there's no life here. I tried to be a success five times, and five times I was ruined. And what do you think I was looking for, eh? What? A day's wage, food for Olga and me. Over there in Australia, you're sure of food. So they say. With twelve thousand drachmas, you're saved. If I could only win three times on Misiri, Asian and Chrisoula... But there you go. Last Sunday at the races, I won a hundred and twenty drachmas. I'm going down there again, but Pericles is being substituted. Just my luck. Mr El Kempir was going to ride him. There goes my forecast, and there goes the hundred and twenty, as you can see.

STRATOS: How much do you want?
STELIOS: Eh?
STRATOS: How much do you want?
STELIOS: Wait a minute. I didn't mean to...
STRATOS: It'll be a loan.
STELIOS: Again? It isn't right!
STRATOS: Between ourselves now.
STELIOS: I owe you a packet already.
STRATOS: As if you weren't going to give it back to me.
STELIOS: Of course I'll give it back to you.
STRATOS: Will fifty drachmas do? (*He gives the fifty drachma note to him.*)
STELIOS (*taking it quickly, and putting it into his pocket*): I was just the same. I would lend to everybody. And look at me now. *You should be more careful. I'm speaking to you as an older man.*
DORA: Damn this fly.
STELIOS: A fly? (*He gets up full of spirit, very happy.*)
DORA: It's been bothering me, and won't leave me alone.
STELIOS: But how could he tear himself away from your sweet thighs? Ah, if only I were a fly... or the lace on your panties. Isn't that so, Strato? Dora fancies you. Did you know that?
DORA: Liar.
STELIOS: Listen to her! She's ashamed, don't you see? "That man," she said to me, "My God, what a man." He has only to glance at you, and you're his slave. You just want to wash his feet and wipe them with your hair. That's what she said, word for word.
DORA: Watch your tongue, you old liar. You're too familiar. (*She gathers up her things to leave.*)
STELIOS: Stop shouting now. You think he's like me? "If only I had the money to buy her a villa of white coral." That's what he

ACT TWO

said to me. He's keen, but she's playing hard to get.
(DORA *leaves angrily*.)
STRATOS: You've gone too far again.
STELIOS: It's all right. I was only having a joke ... seeing as how I'm leaving. I'll have to tell Olga, but I'll be in trouble. Luckily she doesn't worry anymore when I disappear. (*Laughing*): She knows me too well by now. (*Going out*): The things she's gone through ... God forgive me. (*He leaves hastily*.)
OLGA (*comes down from the back, takes a look at the street, and then walks over to* STRATOS): Where's he going?
STRATOS: I don't know.
OLGA: Why did you lend him money again?
STRATOS: I did not!
OLGA: I saw you.
STRATOS: OK. I lent him money.
OLGA: You promised me you wouldn't lend him anything again.
STRATOS: I feel sorry for him.
OLGA: Lending him money makes it worse.
STRATOS: Why? He believes he'll win someday.
OLGA: You're lying. You don't lend him money because you're sorry for him. You do it to get rid of him, to get him away.
STRATOS: That's your opinion.
OLGA: I don't want to see you humiliate him like this. Do you hear? I don't want it.
STRATOS: Do you think I can listen to him whining at my feet for fifty drachmas?
OLGA: Let him die, but don't humiliate him like this. It's shameful. It's vile.
STRATOS: How did you see me humiliating him?
OLGA: How do you feel every time you put your hand in your pocket to give him money, eh? Do you think I can't guess what you're feeling, and what you're saying to yourself?
STRATOS: What do you want me to do?
OLGA: Stop paying him. That's what I want. It's as if you're paying for *me*.
STRATOS: What did you say? Have you gone mad?
OLGA: You don't have to. Do you understand! You don't even have to speak to him or look at him. I see you keeping him company out here, and I choke with shame. I want to die. You must leave here ... leave. He's my husband. I don't want you to humiliate him like this. Who do you think you are?

STRATOS: I've never humiliated him — never. I behave toward him as well as I can. He even thinks I lend him money out of respect. He's going on all the time about how I'm his best friend.

OLGA: How can you stand hearing him say that?

STRATOS: He says it.

OLGA: Aren't you ashamed? He sees you as his friend. He sees *me* as ... and the two of us are ...

STRATOS: We'll go away *together*.

OLGA: He's good ... good ... he's the best man in the whole world.

STRATOS: Good ... good ... where's his goodness? He's a gambler, a sponger — that's what he is. I'm not letting you waste your life. Do you hear? I'm not letting you do it even if I have to kill him.

OLGA: It was all right before you came along.

STRATOS: And if I hadn't come, you'd have stayed here until you died.

OLGA: So, I'd have died! It would've been better than you coming here the way you did.

STRATOS: It was better for *me*, I can tell you! You've made a new man of me. Before I met you, all I did was go out with my friends. I didn't give a damn about anything. I couldn't have cared less about women. I was with a different one every night, and now I'm stuck here waiting for hours to exchange a stolen glance with you. You've made me see everything differently.

(*A pause.*)

OLGA: Where's he going?

STRATOS: To the café ... to the races. God knows where after that. It'll be midnight before he gets back. Let's go.

(*Olga does not reply.*)

STRATOS: Olga.

(*Olga still does not reply.*)

STRATOS: Yesterday, I went there and sat alone for hours. I thought I heard your laughter. If your laughter were pebbles or sprigs of thyme, I could gather them and cherish them ... that's what I was thinking.

OLGA: I'll go and get dressed. I'll go out first by the back door.

STRATOS: All right.

(OLGA *leaves.* STRATOS, *looking pleased, goes up to* JORDAN.)

STRATOS: Mr Jordan. I want to treat you.

JORDAN (*looking rather stern*): *You* to treat *me*?

ACT TWO

STRATOS: Yes, you. I'll treat you to whatever you like.
JORDAN: You very young to treat *me*!
STRATOS: Why? (*He goes up two steps of the stairway.*)
JORDAN: Don't set foot on my stairs.
STRATOS: What harm will it do?
JORDAN: I don't want you set foot on stairs. Take feet off.
STRATOS: Why are you shouting at me? Have I ever annoyed you?
JORDAN: Mind your own business.
STRATOS: Pity. I like you.
JORDAN: Listen to that. He treat *me*. (*He makes a dismissive sound.*) When I said I treat *you*, why you say no, eh? (*He makes dismissive sound again.*) Now mind your own business, and me mine!
STRATOS: Why not? (*He looks at his watch, and goes into his apartment.*)
JORDAN: Hey, Yanni! Where is Yannis?
(STELIOS *comes into the yard with the suitcase and bundle that* BABIS *had taken when he was leaving. He puts them on the ground.*)
STELIOS (*calling out discreetly towards the street*): Babi, come on.
BABIS (*coming slowly into the courtyard, looking towards the back*): Is she in?
STELIOS: She is. Sit down.
(*They sit down somewhere.*)
BABIS: Cigarette?
STELIOS: Thanks. I have a light. (*He lights their cigarettes.*)
BABIS: Thanks, Stelio. So he goes to a grocer's and asks for pepper. They give him unground peppercorns. "*Ground* pepper," he says. They haven't got it. He goes to another grocer's. "Pepper," he says. Again they give it to him unground. "Is it ground?" Here they tell him, "Everybody buys it like this, and grinds it themselves." He's a sly one. A real Greek.
STELIOS: Clever.
(STELIOS *and* BABIS *laugh with satisfaction.*)
STELIOS: He hires ten Africans, buys ten mortars and pestles, and tells them to grind the pepper. He puts it in little transparent envelopes — like you see in Athena Street, and begins to trade. Eh, the ten mortars and pestles become twenty, the twenty fifty, the fifty a hundred, the hundred a thousand, and then the thousand . . .
BABIS: How many?

STELIOS: No, you tell *me*.
BABIS: Two thousand.
STELIOS: A factory with ten thousand workers.
BABIS: Well, what do you know!
STELIOS: Today, he's one of the richest men in Venezuela. That's the trick — to hit on a good idea, and a good machine, then build a factory.
BABIS: In Australia, it's even better than in Venezuela.
STELIOS: Much better. They found the biggest diamond in the world there.
BABIS: And if we went to the outback as you were saying . . .
STELIOS: The outback — the virgin lands.
BABIS: Give me a place to live. Give me a piece of land I could swoop down on. If you could only see what these hands are capable of!
STELIOS: You should see what mine can do!
BABIS: We're off!
STELIOS: We're off!
   (STRATOS *comes out of his room ready to go out.*)
STRATOS (*seeing* STELIOS *and* BABIS): You've come back?
STELIOS: What do you mean? We're off together. (*Putting his arm around* BABIS's *shoulder*): Aren't we, Babi?
BABIS: We certainly are.
STRATOS: Where to?
STELIOS: To Australia. In two months at the most. I can see you at Piraeus, waving your handkerchief from the quay.
BABIS: In two months at the most.
STRATOS: I always said you'd come up with a winning hand.
STELIOS: And I said so too — but I found Babis at the corner and . . .
BABIS: Stelios and I have eaten bread and salt together. We're really friends, even though we annoy each other sometimes . . .
STELIOS: We're only human. Here are your fifty drachmas.
STRATOS: Forget it. Keep it.
STELIOS: Take it. I didn't need it.
STRATOS: You'll need it this afternoon.
STELIOS: Never mind about that. Cards are no way out.
STRATOS: I said keep it. You can give it back to me with the rest.
STELIOS: All right. I'll keep it. Are you going somewhere?
STRATOS: Yes, I'm going out for a walk. What can I do in here on my own?

ACT TWO

STELIOS: Take care. Have a good evening. Have you found yourself a little charmer? How did you manage that, you dark horse? I'm serious, now. I'll see you in Piraeus with a box of Turkish Delight down at the quay.
(STRATOS *leaves*.)
STELIOS: A good young man. A man of few words, but good. Babi, I'm with you. One minute till I tell Olga I'm here.
VOULA (*coming from the back, dressed to go out*): Where are you going? Olga's gone out.
STELIOS: Gone out? Where?
VOULA: I don't know. She got dressed and went out.
STELIOS: She didn't say where she was going?
VOULA: See if she told Maritsa. She doesn't tell *me* anything!
STELIOS: Why does she never say? (*He goes to the back*.)
(VOULA *goes towards the street*. BABIS *glances at her*.)
BABIS: Where in the name of God are you going?
VOULA: I'm leaving too.
BABIS: You've forgotten to bring your things with you.
VOULA: Give them to somebody else. I don't want them.
BABIS: Fine. Now cook us something to eat.
VOULA: Cook for yourself. Forget about me.
BABIS: I'll get dirty. I'm wearing my best suit.
VOULA: My heart bleeds. (*She goes to leave*.)
(BABIS *grabs her by the arm, and embraces her*.)
BABIS: There's just one thing I want to say. I went as far as the corner, and felt so lonely. Just think, I could have kept going. I sat down at the corner on purpose, so that somebody would find me and say: "Ah now, go back home to your girl. Where are you off to, you idiot? Idiots leave the women they love, and disappear. Come on, Babi. Go back home."
VOULA: Do you want a salad?
BABIS: I want *you*.
STELIOS (*coming from the back looking thoughtful*): She didn't even tell Maritsa. She put on her best clothes and went off.
(VOULA *goes to lift* BABIS's *suitcase*.)
BABIS: Leave it. I'll take it.
VOULA (*softly*): Tell Stelios to come and eat with us. (*She goes off to their apartment*.)
STELIOS: She's not to blame. She'll have thought that I wasn't coming till the evening, and that's why she went off.
BABIS: I'm sure that's it, otherwise she'd have stayed at home.

STELIOS: She wouldn't have put a foot out of the house before, without telling me. But now it's getting worse all the time with us. Do you understand? She's angry with me, especially since that evening when there was the fight about the twenty drachmas. I went down in her estimation. Do you understand? I went down so far. Now, I'm a piece of rubbish. And since Stratos gave him a thump... why so much fuss over that? *I* could have given it. But because he did it instead, she talks about *him* all the time. You'd think he was the aristocracy. Do you see how low I appear in her eyes? Because of this, I have to get back my self-esteem. We must go to Australia.

BABIS: I've decided, once and for all!

STELIOS: We'll go together. Give me your hand.

(STELIOS *and* BABIS *clasp hands*.)

BABIS: With the help of God!

STELIOS: With the help of God!

BABIS: United we stand!

STELIOS: We'll work like dogs to begin with. Agreed?

BABIS: Agreed!

STELIOS: We'll not spend five drachmas until we've made a pile. And then, we'll start looking for a good machine.

BABIS: Like the one for grinding the pepper.

STELIOS: I'll find more than that! Not just one, ten or a hundred. I'll find a thousand! Let me get out of here where I'm crushed by so many problems, where they're calling me a sponger... a fool. Once I've set foot on new ground, you'll see what I'm made of. Then, Babi — you won't have to worry. We'll be saved.

BABIS: That's what I say... we'll be saved.

STELIOS (*with deep relief*): Thank God.

LIGHTS OUT

ACT THREE

Six weeks later. It is evening. OLGA *is alone in the courtyard. Suddenly, she gets up and gazes happily towards the street.* STRATOS *come in.*

OLGA: Why are you late this evening?
STRATOS: It's the first time you've ever said that.
OLGA: Don't you like it?
STRATOS: Say it as many times as you want, and any way you want. What's happened to make you care so much?
OLGA: I was waiting for you.
STRATOS: You weren't waiting for me the other evenings?
OLGA: I've waited for you every time!
STRATOS: Then why did you never say a word?
OLGA: This evening is different! Don't you feel it?
STRATOS (*looking around*): They're all out?
OLGA: They are. It's quiet, isn't it?
STRATOS: I wonder why that is?
OLGA: Isn't it nice?
STRATOS: You'd think a big machine had stopped. How did such a miracle happen?
OLGA: As soon as Babis and Voula left, the others scattered as if they were being hunted. You'd have thought the place couldn't hold them.
STRATOS: So, they got away, did they?
OLGA: You should've seen it! We were all crying.
STRATOS: So they've gone. Now, she'll be sitting on his knee on the deck of the ship, and they'll be talking about Australia.
OLGA: Only *he* wasn't here.
STRATOS: Where is he?
OLGA: I don't know. He's been very busy since midday.
STRATOS: Then . . . it's only the two of us here now?
OLGA: Yes, and before you came, I was here alone — very alone. I can't remember ever feeling like that here before. That's why I thought you were late! I felt it so much that I waited for you — in this stifling yard. Do you remember me ever sitting here like this as the others do?
STRATOS: No!

OLGA: Never! I loathe it. It's my hell. And yet while I was waiting for you, it could have been a palace. I felt for it. I loved it... this place... because I had the joy of knowing that you would come.

STRATOS (*rubs his face and the nape of his neck restlessly*): They have their arms round each other on the deck. They're gazing at the sea, breathing the fresh air. They're throwing their cigarette butts into the waves, and talking about Australia. What's the use of you waiting for me? They'll all come back soon, and we'll be choking on insults and filth again.

OLGA: I give you whatever happiness I can. What more can I do?

STRATOS: Why aren't you waiting for me in our house, our own house, the house belonging to the two of us?

OLGA: No!

STRATOS: Olga, listen! No woman has ever said the things you've said to me. No other words have ever warmed my heart like yours, not even my mother's. But I don't want to hear the words you say to me in *this* place. It's as if they fall to the ground and Asta, Jordan and your husband trample on them with their dirty feet.

OLGA: I can't leave him!

STRATOS: Open your eyes. See him for what he is. He's worthless. He's rubbish... a loser. If he were playing cards, and they told him "Your wife has left you", he'd go on playing. He'd gamble you away for a few thousand drachmas.

OLGA: You only think that, because you don't know him. But he was crying all last night.

STRATOS: *He* was crying?

OLGA: Whimpering like a baby.

STRATOS: Why?

OLGA: He was saying that our life was ruined, that *he* was to blame, that if only he could begin all over again.

STRATOS: What came over him?

OLGA: It was because the others were leaving. He wanted to leave too. "They've saved themselves," he said. "They've saved themselves," and he was crying.

STRATOS: He wants to go and find money for gambling. And then what? He'd leave *you* here and never give a damn what happened to you.

OLGA: He loves me.

STRATOS: Yes, but you love *me*!

ACT THREE

OLGA: If I leave him, he'll be totally lost. As long as I'm with him . . .

STRATOS: I don't believe you. Do you know how much money I've lent him since the day he got this idea into his head about going to Australia? One thousand five hundred drachmas! Fifteen hundred-drachma notes. And do you know on what understanding I gave him a hundred drachmas every day? That he'd go and play cards, then come back at midnight. Don't you understand? He, my love, knows that there's something between us, but for a hundred drachmas, it's all right. That's how much of a pimp he is. And you're calling him an angel? You pity him?

OLGA: No. He knows nothing. He suspects nothing.

STRATOS: And if he's the kind of person I say he is, then what'll you do?

OLGA: Whatever you want me to do!

STRATOS: The two of us'll get away from here.

OLGA: Yes!

STRATOS: I work like a dog. I don't spend a five drachma piece, and I'm earning plenty. Look. (*He gives her an account book.*) I've just put another two thousand in the bank. I work like a dog. I've never done so much, or worked so well.

(STELIOS *comes in. He stops short. He is surprised to see them close together like this. There is a pause. They see him, and are agitated. There is something about their behaviour that betrays them.* OLGA *is still holding* STELIOS's *bankbook.*)

STELIOS: Good evening. (*He leaves a packet he was holding on the steps.*)

STRATOS: Good evening.

OLGA: Where were you?

STELIOS: Stop asking where I was all the time. I'm a man. I was where I wanted to be. Am I asking *you* what you're doing here?

OLGA: What do you see me doing?

STELIOS (*seems afraid, but tries to make a joke out of the situation*): Just what I thought! Didn't I see for myself? You're doing nothing. You're just having a chat.

OLGA: Then why are you shouting?

STELIOS (*to* STRATOS): I have her badly trained. If I say a cross word to her, she's all hurt.

STRATOS: You do tend to pass remarks once in a while. I've told you that before!

STELIOS: I've not been feeling a hundred percent lately. I'll go and

THE COURTYARD OF WONDERS

freshen myself up a bit. (*He goes to the back.*)

OLGA: We must get away from here. But how can we?

STRATOS: I'll sort it out. You'll see!

OLGA: How?

STRATOS: I'll tell him everything honestly and plainly . . . like a man! It won't bother him at all. I promise you. He'll be relieved when you go. I'm telling you, and you'll remember what I said.

OLGA: Not yet. Don't say anything. Please.

STRATOS: It's wrong to delay things — wrong to torment ourselves.

OLGA: If I could only believe that it wouldn't bother him . . .

STRATOS: Let me speak to him, and you'll see. It's best to do it now, when the others are away, and just the three of us are here. Whatever happens, nobody else'll hear it. Nobody else'll know about it.

OLGA: I don't *want* to.

STRATOS: Why?

OLGA: If he were the kind of man you think he is, he'd never have said a word. He wouldn't have been angry. Did you see how he reacted just now when he saw us together? He suspects, and he's suffering. Don't you see?

STRATOS: He has suspicions, the pathetic little man, but he isn't suffering. That's the difference. He's only keeping up appearances so that he can take more from me. You know how much I've lent him altogether?

OLGA: I don't want to know!

(ANNETO *comes in. As soon as she sees them, she begins to sing "Romona". She goes up the ladder, unlocks the door to the loft, and crawls in.*)

OLGA: I must go in now.

STRATOS: Stay for a moment, otherwise the old woman'll be suspicious.

OLGA: We must go away. We must!

(ANNETO *throws some rubbish down out of the loft.* STRATOS *sees her.*)

STRATOS (*enraged*): Tell me, do you do that kind of thing in England?

ANNETO: This isn't England. This is Athens.

STRATOS: Listen here, you old witch. I'm telling you for the last time. If you throw rubbish at my door again, I'll grab you, and throw you into the river!

ACT THREE

ANNETO: We can discuss it all the day after tomorrow in court. Don't be in such a hurry.
OLGA: Let her be. Don't speak to her.
ANNETO: Why shouldn't he speak to me, tsarina? Have you a monopoly on him?
OLGA: Have you gone off your head?
STRATOS: I respect your years. If you were any younger, I'd sort you out.
ANNETO: Keep your respect for married women, even though they're young.
OLGA: What are you driving at?
ANNETO (*to* OLGA): Do you want me to say it?
(OLGA *runs away upset*.)
ANNETO: She's off!
STRATOS: Why the hell are you always quarrelling with me? What's your problem?
ANNETO: Go and ask my solicitor. 1D Santaroza Street.
STRATOS: Who threw this rubbish here in front of my door?
ANNETO: It's not your door, it's mine!
STRATOS: Have I rented the room or haven't I? Didn't I pay you the rent and the deposit as you asked?
ANNETO: So what? Did you rent it for eight hundred years?
STRATOS: For one year. I've been here for four months, and I'll stay for another six.
ANNETO: What are you going on about, man? Did we make a contract for a year?
STRATOS: Yes, we did!
ANNETO: Where's the document? Show me the document.
STRATOS: We didn't draw up a document. We gave our word!
ANNETO: Words aren't binding.
STRATOS: Mine are.
ANNETO: In England, we recognise only documents.
MARIA (*coming out*): What's going on again in the pigeon loft?
STRATOS: How did you put up with her for so many years without strangling her?
ANNETO: Go and drown yourself!
MARIA: What sort of talk is that? Aren't you ashamed, old woman?
ANNETO: Are *you* not ashamed, roaming about from morning till night when your husband's away?
MARIA: Everybody knows where I go.
ANNETO: Maybe they do, but those marks on your neck — nobody

knows where *they* came from.

MARIA: I hurt myself.

ANNETO: Did you hurt your lips? Those are kiss marks.

MARIA: Did you have a good look at them?

ANNETO: Why are you hiding them, eh? Show them to us. Shall I come down? Will you let me see them? Stay there. I'm on my way down.

MARIA: Do you think I'd let *you* examine me?

ANNETO (*sings*): "Romona, I hear the mission bells above ..."

(MARIA *walks over, and takes away the ladder.*)

ANNETO: Where are you taking the ladder?

MARIA: Now you can't come down. You can die up there.

ANNETO: Take it. Take it. (*She sings louder than before*): "Romona, they're singing out our song of love."

(MARIA *submissively puts the ladder back in place, and goes to the back.*)

ANNETO: That's her gone, too! (*She goes into the loft.*)

STELIOS (*comes from the back*): Six o'clock. It's six o'clock already. Would you believe it? They'll have done about sixty miles by now. The ship left at three o'clock. A fine ship, it can do twenty miles an hour. On the twenty first of the month they'll be in Australia.

MARIA: What happened to you? Babis was asking for you ... and Voula.

STELIOS: Were they really asking for me?

MARIA: Of course. They were worried. They were wondering what could have happened to you.

OLGA: You talked about going to Australia together, and you didn't even say goodbye to them. You didn't show up. You're all talk.

STELIOS: No, Olga. Look here. (*He shows her a packet he is carrying. He opens it.*)

OLGA: What's that?

STELIOS: Turkish Delight and almond cakes. I went to find some Turkish Delight. That's why I was late. I didn't want to say goodbye to them empty handed.

OLGA: Why did you disappear? You knew they were leaving here at two o'clock.

STELIOS: But I went to Piraeus, Olga. I looked for them. I searched the customs, but couldn't find them. I couldn't find them anywhere. I begged and pleaded with the sailors and officers to let me get onto the ship, but they wouldn't. I'd give them the

ACT THREE

Turkish Delight, and leave the ship immediately — but no. "Please, come with me so's I can give the present to them and say goodbye." It was no good. "Do me a favour. *You* give it them, and tell them from Stelios not to think he's a swine." They wouldn't do it.

MARIA: Did you not even see them in the distance? Weren't they on the deck when the ship was leaving?

STELIOS: I couldn't see very well. There were so many people. At one point, I was shouting, "Safe journey." I was shouting, "Babi, Voula!" I was waving my handkerchief and the sweets. I think they'd have seen me.

MARIA: They would certainly have seen you.

STELIOS: Do you think so? *I* couldn't see very well.

MARIA: They'll have seen you, don't worry. Babis has telescopic sight.

STELIOS (*regretfully*): Ah, Babi . . .

OLGA: Have you eaten?

STELIOS: I'm not hungry. Olga, look at this! I've brought you Turkish Delight and almond cakes. I bring good stuff, don't I? You never get any rubbish from me!

(*Slightly irritated,* OLGA *takes the two boxes, and goes to the back.*)

STELIOS: She's fond of sweet things, you know. At one time, I used to bring her sweets regularly from the best confectioners. She still has the boxes. She keeps buttons and spools of thread and little bottles in them. That's all that's left. Empty chocolate and glacé fruit boxes . . . empty boxes.

STRATOS: Do you remember saying that I'd come down to Piraeus with a box of Turkish Delight to see you off? You went instead, and you were left high and dry.

STELIOS: You think I won't go? In two or three months, I'll be sailing off, don't you worry. Maybe it's better that Babis has gone first. That way, I'll have a base when I arrive. Do you know what he said to me? He'll send me the first money he makes, so's my papers can be brought forward.

STRATOS: You'll have to give up *you know what* when you get over there.

STELIOS: What?

STRATOS: The cards. What else?

STELIOS: You think I *like* playing?

STRATOS: You'll be working day and night in Australia. It won't matter whether you like to play or not.

STELIOS: Only God knows what I go through when I open a pack of cards. My heart beats fit to burst. I can't breathe properly, and I'm in a cold sweat! Do you know what they call me at the café?

STRATOS: How would I know?

STELIOS: The Ghost! The Ghost... because I go white. They think I go white with the thrill of the game, with my passion for it. But ask me, and I'll tell you what tortures I go through when I play. I'm ready to faint. I hate cards. Don't you understand? I hate cards, and the people who play them.

STRATOS: Then why do you play?

STELIOS: How else can I make a living? I opened three shops, and they all closed. Now I'm a clerk in the Ministry of Commerce. The government might change tomorrow. Then they'll say, "Throw out these clerks. Take in others." I play to try and fulfil my dream. That's why I play. I want twelve thousand drachmas, so's I can go to Australia. Where'll I find it if I don't play?

STRATOS: But you're always losing.

STELIOS: I lose, but I still play — and as long as you keep playing, you keep hoping, whereas if you do nothing...

STRATOS: Once you get to Australia, with God's help, you must forget the cards.

STELIOS: I will, Strato, I will!

ASTA (*coming in from outside*): Good evening. (*She goes towards the back.*)

STRATOS: Good evening.

STELIOS: I will, Strato. I'll give them up. You'll see. Isn't it a strange thing?

STRATOS: What?

STELIOS: I was just thinking. Will you laugh at me if I tell you what I'm thinking?

STRATOS: *I* don't laugh easily.

STELIOS: I believe I'm a clever man. I'm worth something. I know a lot of things. I have abilities. I'm a very wise and practical person, honest and straight — as they say. I'm a very decent, admirable man. You'll say to me, "Where are all these qualities? I don't see them." I agree. I don't see them either. But as soon as I set foot in Australia, you'll see them all. I know I can be something. I think I'll even know the language from the very first day. That's why I have to go. Do you understand? I *have* to.

STRATOS: And... your wife?

ACT THREE

STELIOS: She'll come and find another man... the kind she dreamed of when she was a girl.
STRATOS: And until she goes, what'll she live on here?
STELIOS: I'll arrange everything before I leave. I haven't thought about it yet, but I'll see to it.
(OLGA *comes in from the back, and goes towards the street.*)
STELIOS: We were just saying...
OLGA: I'm going out for a while.
STELIOS: Where are you off to?
OLGA: I won't be long!
STELIOS: What is this? Is it not right and proper to tell me where you're going?
OLGA: I said I won't be long.
STELIOS: OK, all right. I asked out of...
(OLGA *goes out.*)
STELIOS: Did you see that? I have her badly trained. I've never struck my fist on the table like a man. I'm a civilized person. I wanted my wife to be a lady, you know what I mean?
STRATOS: Do you still love her?
STELIOS: As soon as I set foot in Australia, I'll love her again, as I did at first.
STRATOS: So... you don't love her now?
STELIOS: The magic's faded. You know what I mean? We've spoiled everything. I'm speaking to you like a brother again. She's half Russian. Did you know that?
STRATOS: So I've heard.
STELIOS: She was beautiful. She was different. I loved her the moment I saw her. I still had the shop then. I *was* something. I went out with her for weeks. I spent plenty on her... and then she said yes. She brought me to see her parents. They were still alive then, God forgive them. They spoke Russian among themselves. They had a samovar for making tea, and they'd give me Russian food — salad with pork, beetroot soup and things like that. Her mother called her Olya. We got married in the Russian church. You should have seen it. A choir... and the church full of aristocrats — fallen of course — but aristocrats all the same. I married above me, you know what I mean? And what was *I*? My old man was a waiter at the Olympia restaurant. We did well at first, but then I lost the shop. I was broke. And my wife was above me. Don't you see? I had to economise, so's not to go downhill. So that she wouldn't think I was useless and

incapable, that she had made a mistake in marrying me. But there was no saving me from the worst — from poverty to more poverty, and on top of that, knowing that she despised me. Never marry above you. Do you hear? Never! It's torture. It's hell. She becomes a tyrant. Little by little, your love goes to the devil. You're frightened of her . . . and then without realising it, you hate her . . . you detest her.

STRATOS: So she was bad to you?

STELIOS: She never said a word against me. Not one! She didn't need to. Couldn't I see for myself that she was wasted on me? Was I a fool to drag her into this courtyard? Didn't I know what she would think?

STRATOS: You hate her, then?

STELIOS: I don't wish her ill, no. I wish her well. As soon as I set foot in Australia, everything'll change. I'll pay you back what I owe . . . in full.

STRATOS: Don't worry about it. Why think about that?

STELIOS: Of course I'll pay. I owe it to you.

STRATOS: *I've* written it off.

STELIOS: Why? Do you take me for a sponger who grabs handouts and then clears off?

STRATOS: Not at all, but between the two of us, we needn't worry about a few hundred. That's what I wanted to say. And whenever you want any more, just ask me.

STELIOS: I wouldn't have the face to. I owe you so much.

STRATOS: Do you want some more?

STELIOS: There are some suckers at the café who've earned good money. Here, look. (*He takes out a notebook.*) I've noted everything down . . . yours and the others. Stratos — debit one thousand five hundred drachmas. Malamatas — debit one hundred and fifty drachmas. Maritsa — debit two hundred and thirty drachmas. Anneto — two hundred. All with their dates. A correct account. I'm showing you this, so that you don't think that . . .

STRATOS: I know, and that's why I'm saying that whenever you want more, all you have to do is ask . . . even now if you need it.

STELIOS: No.

STRATOS: Since I know you haven't a drachma . . . (*He takes out some money to give him.*)

STELIOS: I've told you I don't want it.

(STRATOS *puts the note into* STELIOS's *pocket.* ANNETO *glances*

ACT THREE

down furtively from the loft.)
STRATOS: Take it. Take it, and don't say a word.
STELIOS: Why do you keep insisting? I tell you, I don't want it. (*He takes the note out of his pocket.*)
STRATOS: Stop acting coy. I know you'll take it in the end. (*He puts the note into* STELIOS's *pocket again.*)
STELIOS: I mustn't get into debt.
STRATOS (*catching* STELIOS's *hand as he goes to take the note out of his pocket again*): Will you stop it? Since when did you become shy? (*He gives him a friendly slap on the back.*) Good for you! When you go to Australia, you can pay it all back in one go.
STELIOS (*gets up*): I must get to Australia. I must.
ASTA (*comes from the back*): Mr Stelio.
STELIOS: Leave me alone, and you'll live to enjoy your children. I've my own troubles.
ASTA: Who can I talk to? *You* know...
STELIOS: Why do you come to me with your problems? Whatever moan you have, you load it onto me, as if I were the Holy Mother... the consoler. What do you take me for? Do you think I'm here to console others?
(ANNETO *comes out the door of the loft.*)
ASTA: *You* know...
STELIOS: I know nothing! You've taken me for an educated person, and you want me to solve your problems. Well, I'm telling you once and for all. I'm not educated, and your moaning hardly needs to be analysed. Go on. Leave me alone. I've business to attend to.
ANNETO: He has a rendezvous with the Queen of Spades. Didn't you see him taking the pieces of silver to betray — just like Judas?
STELIOS: Who's speaking to you?
STRATOS (*to* STELIOS): Go about your business. Don't pay any attention to her!
ANNETO: The day after tomorrow, in court, I'll tell you which women he shouldn't pay attention to.
STELIOS: At the court, I'll teach you how to behave yourself!
ANNETO: First bring me the two hundred you owe me, and then you can teach me how to behave! Worthless, lying witness! Fool!
STRATOS: Give it to her. (*He takes out some money, and gives it*

to him.)
STELIOS: From you? No!
STRATOS: It's shameful for that worm to have you in her hand.
(STELIOS *grabs the money from* STRATOS's *hand, and goes to climb up to the loft.*)
ANNETO: You've sold out.
(STELIOS *hesitates. He looks at one, and then the other, not knowing what to do.*)
STRATOS: Give it to her, will you?
ANNETO: False witness. You've completely sold out!
STELIOS: That'll do. I'll owe her. (*He puts the money into* STRATOS's *hand, and goes out to the back.*)
ANNETO: He's off.
STRATOS: Do you know what you look like up there? A viper! (*He locks his door.*)
ANNETO: Don't worry. I haven't bitten anyone yet! I'm keeping my poison for you.
STRATOS: Watch you don't swallow it. (*He goes out towards the street.*)
ASTA: It's shameful.
ANNETO (*coming down from the loft*): Am I to blame? We never heard the like of that in England.
(JORDAN *comes in carrying a stew pot with a handle that he takes his food in when he goes to work.*)
ASTA: Jordan, listen. Listen.
JORDAN (*without looking at her*): Eh?
ASTA: They came again today, and measured us.
JORDAN: Who?
ASTA: The surveyors!
JORDAN (*turns towards her, and looks her straight in the eye.*): When?
ASTA: This morning! A whole lot of them came, about five or six.
ANNETO: Six!
ASTA: First two, then three, and today six surveyors.
(JORDAN *sits down on the steps, as if burdened by a heavy weight.*)
ASTA: And they brought a machine today.
JORDAN: What machine?
ASTA: A thing like a telescope, and the one with the glasses and the trilby was looking at us for an hour through it.
ANNETO: He wasn't looking at us. He was looking at the pole.

ACT THREE

JORDAN (*takes his wife's hand, and pulls her gently towards him*): Come here.

(JORDAN *and* ASTA *sit side by side.*)

JORDAN: What pole was he looking at?

ASTA: A big, long one with black numbers and red numbers all over it.

ANNETO: One of them was holding the pole, and the other was looking through the telescope. The one that was holding the pole was cross-eyed.

ASTA: Yoakim went over to them — he's only a child — he went over to them to see what they were doing, and the one with the trilby gave him a slap with the back of his hand. The poor child was giddy with it.

JORDAN: What did they say?

ASTA: Nothing. They spoke only to each other.

JORDAN: What were they talking about?

ASTA: Numbers.

(JORDAN *has a dark, fixed expression on his face. His eyes have a withdrawn look.*)

ANNETO: You'll see. Sooner or later, we'll be packing up and moving somewhere else, and when we pass by here again, we won't know our street. Everything will have gone — our apartments, the steps. Even the ground we walk on will have been taken, and thrown away who knows where. They'll have put a luxury apartment block on top of the courtyard. Strange to think of it, eh?

ASTA: Where'll *we* go?

ANNETO: The ones who've been living here since before 1950 will get compensation. Maritsa and I will get something. A pity you didn't come here before 1950.

(JORDAN *gets up.*)

ASTA: What do you want?

(JORDAN *doesn't speak. Without turning towards her, he touches* ASTA*'s hair awkwardly with his hand.*)

ASTA: Tell me.

(JORDAN *shakes his head wearily, and goes towards his terrace.*)

ASTA: Jordan.

(JORDAN *goes up to the terrace.* ASTA *gazes after him sorrowfully.*)

ASTA: Will I bring you some wine?

(JORDAN *stays silent.*)

ASTA: Do you want your rifle? There's a whole crowd of cats on the roof.
(JORDAN *stays silent.* STELIOS *comes in from the back.*)
ASTA (*to* STELIOS): They came again today and measured us.
STELIOS: So I heard.
(STELIOS *goes up to the door of* STRATOS's *apartment. He nervously fingers the cross that* STRATOS *was wearing.*)
ASTA (*shouts*): Yoakim! (*She goes out to the street.*)
STELIOS: Strato! Strato! Strato!
ANNETO: He's not here. He went out!
STELIOS: Where did he go?
ANNETO: Don't ask me!
STELIOS: All right then. He was here just now, though.
ANNETO: He made off as soon as you went.
STELIOS: As soon as I went into the house?
ANNETO: Yes. He locked up and went off.
STELIOS: And where did he go?
ANNETO: How would *I* know? He doesn't even tell *you*, and you're his friend — a sorry friendship if I may say so. Do you think he'd tell *me*? But why should he give you an account of himself? Your wife doesn't even tell you where *she* goes.
STELIOS: Eh?
ANNETO: I'm telling you, you don't know how bad your own situation is. You only want to fight with *me*.
(STELIOS *lights a cigarette.* ANNETO *sees the cross he is holding.*)
ANNETO: Is that your cross?
STELIOS: It's his.
ANNETO: Did he give it to you?
STELIOS: He didn't give it to me. Why are you saying that? Did you see him give me anything else?
ANNETO: Isn't he lending you money all the time?
STELIOS: I ask him for it!
ANNETO: And he gives it to you freely, even though he's mean.
STELIOS: Where did you see him being mean?
ANNETO: Have you ever seen him going out to enjoy himself, to spend anything? He sits in here the whole time like the daughter of the house.
STELIOS: He's a quiet man.
ANNETO: What are you talking about? If only you'd open your eyes . . .

ACT THREE

STELIOS (*furious*): Shut up!

ANNETO: What's the matter with you?

STELIOS: Shut up! I can't stand much more . . . there are so many demons in my head. (*He beats his head with his hand.*)

ANNETO: It's not as bad as that. I was only saying . . .

STELIOS: What were you getting at just now? Be honest.

ANNETO: You're the one who's mincing words, not me. If you say an honest word to me first, then I'll say a hundred to you.

STELIOS (*after a pause*): Do you know where I found the cross? In our house, hidden under the paper she puts on the kitchen shelves. Any time I asked him to come in, he wouldn't! So how did the cross get there? She even hid the thing so that I wouldn't see it. So what's happening? Does he go in and out of my house while I'm away?

ANNETO: The day before yesterday . . . just about this time . . . I found them sitting side by side talking.

STELIOS: What? Where were they sitting? Inside?

ANNETO: On the steps here.

STELIOS: Who else was here?

ANNETO: Nobody. Just the two of them.

STELIOS: Just what are you driving at?

ANNETO: Me, nothing. I'm only saying what you fear.

STELIOS: Maybe I'm just imagining things, because of that fight over the twenty drachmas. And then two or three times when she was out, he was out too. And now the cross. And then you found them here.

ANNETO: And he's lending you money all the time.

STELIOS: Are you saying he's pulling the wool over my eyes?

ANNETO: If Olga could only see how worthless he is!

STELIOS: He lends me money on the sly. She doesn't know anything about it.

ANNETO: And I tell you she does know.

STELIOS: Do you think they're in it together?

ANNETO: God knows.

STELIOS: You know a lot more, woman. Tell me!

ANNETO: Are you going to testify against me in court?

STELIOS: I'll do whatever you want. I'll go as your witness.

ANNETO: You know Kiriakos who has the kiosk down at the sea, at Vouliagmeni? He saw them.

STELIOS: What?

ANNETO: He's to blame. She's a saint. Stratos came along when

THE COURTYARD OF WONDERS

she was fed up with you. What do you expect? She's a young woman. I'm not saying they did anything improper. These things happen every day. Olga's young and beautiful. She's had a hard life with you. Her heart yearns for something better. I knew this would happen. I was expecting her to fly off one day and leave you. Then he came along and turned her head.

STELIOS (*jumps up*): You say Kiriakos saw them, eh?

ANNETO: Where're you going?

STELIOS: To speak to him. I want to ask him. I have to know.

ANNETO: Wait a minute.

STELIOS: How will I go? Where will I go?

ANNETO: Stelio, I'm not saying this out of spite towards him. On my daughter's life, I'm telling you for your own good. To stop them laughing at you.

STELIOS: Laughing at me? Laughing at me... eh? So that's it. Everybody thinks I'm a born fool. But I'm not. I'm not. (*He goes out in a distraught state.*)

ANNETO: Stop! (*Frightened*): Now what'll I do? (*She goes over to the loft. She is about to climb the ladder, but changes her mind. She approaches the little terrace. She offers* JORDAN *a cigarette*): Have a cigarette.

(JORDAN *takes one.*)

ANNETO (*giving him a light*): You see? My daughter went and married an Englishman, and left me all alone over here. I nursed her. I brought her up. I gave her my whole life — and what do I get? She threw me to one side and went off with "her Johnny". Why couldn't she have chosen one of our young men? Then I'd have *somebody*. I'd have a house. I'd see my daughter, my grandchildren. I deprive myself by sending her money, so that she can have a dress made, or buy a pair of shoes. That red-faced, sour skinflint gives her next to nothing. Other people say, "How wonderful — she managed to get herself an Englishman." *I* say he can go to hell. When I went to England last year, the insensitive bastard couldn't wait for me to leave. He ate nothing but pudding, and talked about football all evening. He chased me away — you understand — my lord son-in-law. "What am I supposed to do, mother?" that's all she said to me. "What am I supposed to do, mother?" "I know, child," says I. I packed my bundles and came back home. It's important not to lose your husband. When it's finished, you're alone... all alone.

(YANNIS *comes in carrying a case, with* VOULA *following behind*

ACT THREE

him. *She is pale and looks miserable.* YANNIS *puts the case on the ground.* ANNETO *and* JORDAN *haven't seen them.*)

YANNIS (*to* VOULA): Say that you won't leave yet, that you'll go some other time. You see — the yard's not such a bad place.
(VOULA *bursts into tears.* ANNETO *hears them.*)

ANNETO (*almost shrieking*): Voula. Our Voula. (*She runs and hugs her.*) Our Voula. But what happened? Why are you back here again?
(BABIS *comes in carrying two heavy cases. He looks dishevelled and unhappy.*)

ANNETO: Babi!

MARIA (*comes running from the back*): Which Voula? (*She sees her.*) Voula! Babi! You've come back!

ANNETO: What happened? Why are you crying?

MARIA: She's crying? Babi, what's going on? Tell us.

BABIS (*looking around like a madman, as if he cannot keep his eyes on any one place*): They swindled us.

MARIA: Who did?

ANNETO: When? Why?

BABIS: Where's Stelios?

ANNETO: At the kiosk with Kiriakos.

BABIS: Yanni.

YANNIS: Yes, I'll go.

MARIA: Come on. Tell us. What happened?

BABIS: They swindled us.

MARIA: Yes, but who? How did they swindle you? In what way?

BABIS: The one who was going to arrange everything... the one we paid to send us.

ANNETO: But he got the papers for you, the passports. You showed them to me.

BABIS: They were worthless... false. We thought there was something dodgy about them.

ANNETO: Where are the passports? Let's see them.

BABIS: He took them back to get us the tickets. He said he had to show the passports.

MARIA: Did you give him money for the tickets?
(ASTA *comes in from the back.*)

BABIS: All of it. They swindled us.

ASTA (*upset*): Aaaaa.

MARIA: Didn't you suspect anything while you were putting so much money into his hand the second time?

BABIS: I gave him most of it when he bought the passports. Why would I suspect him?
ANNETO: Yes, but that was all a trick.
BABIS: How could I know that?
OLGA (*comes in and looks confused when she sees* VOULA *and* BABIS): Why have you come back?
BABIS: They swindled us, Olga!
MARIA: And then you gave him the money for the tickets?
BABIS: Yes. We were to meet him at the town clock. He was to put us on the ship.
ANNETO: Did you go to the police?
BABIS: We did. They just said, "What can you do? The boat has left."
OLGA: Oh, my God.
ANNETO (*leaves* VOULA, *and hugs* BABIS): You poor children.
VOULA: Babis was going to jump into the sea. Luckily Yannis and I grabbed him. We shouted, and people came running and held him back.
ANNETO: My poor children. My dear children.
OLGA: How could this have happened?
BABIS: You're asking me? You kill yourself to gather the money together. You sell your clothes, your sheets, your wedding rings. You close up your house — only to be ripped off. You see the ship sailing further and further away, and you're left on the quay like a piece of rubbish. She was shouting, "Stop, stop, stop" to the ship like a madwoman . . . like a madwoman.
STELIOS (*running into the courtyard with* YANNIS): Babi. Babi.
BABIS: Stelio, they swindled us.
STELIOS: Eh?
BABIS: They swindled us, Stelio.
STELIOS: Don't tell me . . .
BABIS: The one who was sending us off. Do you hear? The one you said was our saviour.
STELIOS: Babi.
BABIS: He left us standing like fools at the town clock. It was all a trick, Stelio. He disappeared.
STELIOS (*confused*): Disappeared? And you didn't get away? You won't get away then. What? Have I heard right? I don't understand. When *are* you leaving?
BABIS: We won't be leaving. The agent was a swindler. Australia was a trick. He fleeced us.

ACT THREE

STELIOS: A trick? Why? Since Australia is . . . is there. What are you saying? Loads of people leave.
OLGA: Yes, but for these two, there is no journey. It was an illusion.
BABIS: They swindled us.
OLGA: You should've known better!
STELIOS: I'll kill them. Who is he, and where does he live? Tell me! What's that agent's name? Babi, I'll kill him.
OLGA: Be sensible. This is a matter for the police.
STELIOS: It's a matter for me more than anyone. Where does he live? Who is he?
BABIS: I don't know where he lives. If I knew . . .
STELIOS: Where did you find him?
BABIS: At the Alexandra café.
STELIOS: His name?
BABIS: What are you going to do? Do you think he would give me his real name?
STELIOS: Tell me the name he gave you, even if it is false.
OLGA: Forget it. Are you going to try and deal with this yourself?
STELIOS: Why not? Where do you get the idea that I can't? You'll see now what I'm really made of. Babi, in the name of the Holy Mother, why don't you say something? Come on. Come and show him to me. I'll nail him!
(They all laugh sceptically.)
STELIOS: You're laughing, eh? I'm funny, am I? I'm a fool, am I?
VOULA: Leave Babis alone. Can't you see he's half dead?
MARIA *(to* STELIOS): She's right. Go into your apartment, and freshen up. It'll calm you down, and tomorrow, with God's help, you can both look for the man who did this to you. Then, you can deal with him. Where would you go at this time of night?
(A deep sigh from JORDAN, *deep and noisy like the roar of a beast. It makes everyone turn towards the terrace.)*
JORDAN *(speaking in a harsh, monotonous voice, full of pain)*: Go! Go! Go! Go! Go! Go!
MARIA: Come on into my place. You can rest, and then we'll see what happens. Only I haven't any sheets.
ANNETO: I have. *(She goes up to the loft.)*
YANNIS *(lifting the two cases)*: Will I take them to Maria's?
MARIA: Yes, bring them in.
(YANNIS *goes to the back with the two cases.)*
OLGA: Will I make some fried potatoes?

61

MARIA: Let them come and wash first. They need some rest. (*Taking* VOULA *with her*): Come on.
OLGA: I'll give you a dressing gown to change into.
(*The three women go to the back.* BABIS *lifts the third case.*)
STELIOS: Give it to *me*. (*He tries to take it from* BABIS.)
BABIS: Leave it.
STELIOS: I came to Piraeus. I was looking for you. I even brought you Turkish Delight.
BABIS: Ah, Stelio. (*He goes to the back.*)
(ANNETO *comes down from the loft with sheets in her hands.* STRATOS *comes in from outside.* STELIOS *looks fixedly at him.* ANNETO *stays where she is.*)
STELIOS (*to* ANNETO, *boldly and clearly*): I went and asked Kiriakos. It was just as you told me.
ANNETO: Not . . . not now. This isn't the time for arguments.
STRATOS: Why do you want to quarrel?
ANNETO: Don't, Stelio. Not . . . not now.
STELIOS (*to* STRATOS): Tell me. (*He takes the cross out of his pocket.*) Isn't this cross yours?
STRATOS: Where did you find it?
STELIOS: Where do *you* think I found it?
STRATOS: How would *I* know?
(ANNETO *runs to the back.*)
STELIOS: You lost it once, didn't you? You lost it!
STRATOS: I did — two months ago!
STELIOS: And where did you lose it? Where do you think you lost it?
STRATOS: You're talking too much again.
STELIOS: I'm a windbag . . . a chatterbox . . . a talker of rubbish! But I have my rights! If you're a man, you'll tell me where you lost it.
STRATOS: I don't remember.
(MARIA, ANNETO, YANNIS, ASTA *and* VOULA *come in one after the other.*)
STELIOS: Could it have fallen under the paper in the crockery cupboard in our kitchen?
STRATOS: You found it there?
STELIOS: There. Beneath the plates and glasses.
STRATOS: How the hell . . .
STELIOS: I was wondering that too. How the hell . . .
STRATOS: Look here . . . I don't like this kind of nonsense.

ACT THREE

STELIOS: I make no secret of it. I don't like this kind of nonsense either.

STRATOS: Then give me the cross, and be quiet.

STELIOS: First, I'll find out how it came to be in my house, and then I'll give it to you in my own good time. (*Shouting*): Olga! Olga!

(STELIOS *runs to the back.* STRATOS *pushes the others aside, and looks towards the back.* STELIOS *can be heard shouting.*)

STELIOS (*from inside*): How did the cross get here? Tell me, Olga. How did it get here?

OLGA: I don't know.

STELIOS: He gave it to you. Isn't that it? He gave it to you, eh? He gave it to you at Vouliagmeni, eh? When you had a rendezvous down at the sea among the pines . . . eh?

OLGA: Leave me alone. Leave me alone.

STELIOS: Tell me, Olga. I want to know. Tell me about it.

OLGA: Leave me alone. Don't . . . please.

VOULA: My God, what can we do?

STRATOS (*shouting*): Stelio. Listen to me. It's for your own good. Don't touch her. Don't let me hear you upsetting her again. I respect your home, but if you lay a finger on her, you'd better start saying your prayers. Do you hear? Idiot! Sponger! Come outside, and we'll settle this like men.

(*Suddenly, everybody scatters, uttering cries.* STELIOS *comes out from the back. He is holding a knife.* OLGA *is behind him.* STRATOS *calmly steps back.*)

ANNETO: Take the bloody knife away from him.

YANNIS: Mr Stelio.

STELIOS (*to* STRATOS): Here I am.

VOULA (*shouting*): Babi. Where are you?

OLGA: Throw the knife down in front of you!

STELIOS (*to* STRATOS): I'm dealing with this like a man.

(STRATOS *angrily puts his hand in his pocket, and takes out a bundle of notes. He shouts at* STELIOS *as if he were spitting at him.*)

STRATOS: How much do you want, eh? How much?

(*He throws the money in his face.* STELIOS *begins to tremble and cringe with shame and humiliation. The knife falls from his hands. He covers his face, then, bursting into an anguished cry, goes out into the street.*)

LIGHTS OUT

ACT FOUR

One or two months later, on a morning after a night of rain. There are cases and bundles here and there, and a small handcart. In a corner are placed two framed family photographs. JORDAN *is standing motionless and silent on the terrace, wrapped to the ears in an old overcoat. His hands are in his pockets. His gaze is bitter and grim.* SURVEYOR A *and* SURVEYOR B *stride up and down the courtyard talking. As there is continual movement of people in the courtyard, the aesthetic arrangement depends on the director.*

SURVEYOR A: What?
SURVEYOR B: The cars.
SURVEYOR A: Ach mate, don't make a fuss over nothing. Look. From here to here, there are two metres of road to let the cars in and out. When all's said and done, what are you worrying about? In a week or two at the most, you'll be rid of all the rubbish.
SURVEYOR B: Eight or nine days at the most.
SURVEYOR A: Maximum.
(BABIS *comes out from the back with a bundle. He leaves it on the steps. He glances angrily at the two surveyors, and then goes away again to the back. The surveyors continue their conversation.*)
SURVEYOR B: D'you know. That last room, that one there. I think I'll keep it.
SURVEYOR A (*on his own train of thought*): It's not *our* fault. *I* know that.
SURVEYOR B: What isn't?
SURVEYOR A: We notified them two months ago. They should have moved out. Why the hell has it taken them so long? What were you saying?
SURVEYOR B: I'll keep the big apartment for the cement.
SURVEYOR A: Too much trouble. Start building the hut anytime. Whatever happens will happen.
SURVEYOR B: Whatever you like.
(DORA *comes out from the back, and goes towards the street. She is carrying two frying pans, a frilly petticoat and a pair of*

ACT FOUR

black, high-heeled shoes.)
DORA (*shouting*): Did you find the cups?
SURVEYOR A (*to* SURVEYOR B): Come and see this. There's a rock vein coming in here from outside. It must be in this corner.
SURVEYOR B: It doesn't show.
SURVEYOR A: Not here, but you'll come to it about one and a half metres down.
(DORA *comes in from the street, and goes to the back.*)
SURVEYOR B: I'll... (*He looks at* DORA.) I'll get ten labourers from Naxos to clear it with their sledgehammers. Don't worry.
SURVEYOR A: You could do it more quickly with a stick of dynamite. Otherwise we'll be paying wages for days. (*Suddenly, he holds his head.*) Damn this headache.
SURVEYOR B: Have you still got it?
SURVEYOR A: I haven't been able to think or work for a week.
SURVEYOR B: It's the change in the weather; it's the damp. My sister suffers exactly the same way.
(ASTA *comes out from the back, and puts various kitchen utensils on the handcart. She looks at the surveyors with fear.*)
SURVEYOR A (*to* ASTA): How are we getting on? Have we finished?
ASTA: We've finished. We've finished. (*Looking scared, she approaches* JORDAN): Jordan.
(JORDAN *stays silent.*)
ASTA: Jordan, effendi.
(JORDAN *stays silent.*)
ASTA: As if it hasn't happened before — we've seen worse. Why are you so upset this time? Come down from there, effendi.
(JORDAN *doesn't move. He is about to say something, but decides not to.*)
ASTA (*looking at the two surveyors, she moves back one or two steps*): He's right. We're old, and we're still running as if we were under a curse. If we were water, we'd have found a stopping place by now.
SURVEYOR A: I beg your pardon?
ASTA: I was saying...
SURVEYOR A: Aah.
(*The two surveyors go away towards the right.* YANNIS *comes out from the back with a large basket, and his father's old rifle.*)

65

ASTA: What'll we do, Yanni? The old man shows no sign of coming down.

YANNIS (*leaving the things on the handcart*): All right, mother. You go, and don't carry anything else. I'll bring it.

ASTA: That Yoakim...

YANNIS: He's playing outside. Don't worry.

(*In despair*, ASTA *goes out to the back*. YANNIS *approaches the terrace.*)

YANNIS (*to* JORDAN): Your... your rifle, I've just put it on the cart. Why are you being so stubborn? We have so much to talk about. (*He takes out a newspaper cutting.*) The Harbour Commissioners are looking for petty officers. I'm thinking of taking the exams. I wanted to discuss it, to ask you... What do *you* say? What do you think about it?

JORDAN: You're asking me?

YANNIS: If I don't ask you, who can I ask?

JORDAN: Lies, Yanni. Nobody ever asks me.

YANNIS: Eh, how can it be otherwise? Can I do what I please without saying anything to you? When all's said and done, I want your opinion, and if you think I should start the studying... Say something, will you? Why're you ignoring us? What have we done to you? (*On the verge of tears*): Come down. We're all leaving. Everything's packed.

(*The two surveyors come back in.*)

SURVEYOR A (*to* YANNIS): Where can one find some water?

YANNIS: Water?

SURVEYOR A: I want to take an aspirin.

YANNIS: I'll... I'll get it for you. (*He goes out to the back.*)

SURVEYOR A (*looking at the terrace*): What are we going to do about him?

SURVEYOR B: There's something wrong with the old man. We'll find out what the hell he's playing at when the policeman comes.

SURVEYOR A: You said he wasn't to take him by force — just to frighten him a bit.

SURVEYOR B: I told him. There's something wrong with the man. It's strange. (*He goes out.*)

(SURVEYOR A *sits on the steps and writes.*)

ACT FOUR

ANNETO (*stoops while coming out of the loft, and shouts down*): Strato . . . Strato dear . . .
(STRATOS *comes out of his door.*)
ANNETO: Help me to take down the case.
STRATOS: Bring it out!
ANNETO (*her eye falls on* JORDAN): Come down now. You're a sensible man. What good's this doing? We're born refugees. Haven't you realised that yet? What your wife said was right: "If we were water, we'd have found a stopping place by now." (*She gives* STRATOS *a big case.*)
(STRATOS *takes the case and leaves it beside the ladder.*)
ANNETO: If I'd a son like you, I wouldn't want anything else.
(STRATOS, *without replying, goes back into his room.*)
ANNETO: You have children, and England takes them from you. It poured all night. I'll go back to Paros. Where else can I go?
(YANNIS *comes from the back with a glass of water, and a bag. He gives the water to* SURVEYOR A.)
SURVEYOR A: Ah, thanks very much! (*He takes the glass, and goes over to the right.*)
YANNIS: You're welcome! (*He goes to the cart, and puts the bag on it.*)
(DORA *comes out from the back.*)
DORA: Are you here? I was looking for you.
YANNIS (*very moved*): You're off?
DORA: I've said goodbye to everybody — except you.
YANNIS: Does everything fit into the van? Is it all right?
DORA: Yes. You were great finding one so cheap.
YANNIS: He's an acquaintance!
DORA: You won't be running anymore to the shoemaker for my shoes, or for tweezers. You'll be rid of me at last.
YANNIS: I'll remember it all!
DORA: So, what have you decided? Will you sit the exams?
YANNIS: A permanent job as a petty officer isn't bad. It's secure.
DORA: And the uniform'll suit you. Do you know that? Especially in the summer when they wear white.
YANNIS: I couldn't care less about the uniform. I could never stand uniforms. What concerns me is to finish college, and be appointed Harbour Master on one of the islands. And take the

old people with me. You can buy a house for next to nothing in those places. I could put them into a couple of rooms, and say to them, "These are yours." The old man could go fishing for octopus. He loves the best things in life, but he's never been able to have them. He's lived all his life like a hunted man . . . a hunted man.

DORA: I hope everything turns out the way you want. Perhaps I'll visit you sometime one summer.

YANNIS: Whenever you like. You could even come and stay with us . . . forever!

DORA: Don't hope for that.

YANNIS: I'm saying . . .

DORA: You're such a good man.

YANNIS: You . . .

DORA: They've told me at last that they'll be calling me in two weeks at the latest. The one I told you about, the dishy one, said that he's working to get me the supporting role. What do you think? Will I look good on the screen?

YANNIS: I like you just the way you are. I'm not so sure if I'd like you as much on the screen.

DORA: They say I'm photogenic, and that my body . . . ach no, it's not true. Bye-bye. (*She gives him her hand.*)

YANNIS: Bye-bye, Dora.

DORA: We must keep in touch, eh? (*She takes the photographs from the corner, and goes out to the street.*) At last we're getting away from this place.

YANNIS: Give me the photographs. I'll take them.

DORA: No . . . no . . . I can do it.

YANNIS: Dora.

DORA: Yes?

(*There is a short pause.*)

YANNIS: Tell the driver to go slowly. The road's full of potholes because of the rain.

DORA: Don't worry. (*She leaves.*)

(YANNIS *watches* DORA *go. The two surveyors cross the courtyard slowly, talking.*)

SURVEYOR B: There are some nice young girls around these parts.

SURVEYOR A: You don't need to tell me. I like to drive around just

ACT FOUR

to check them out, you know what I mean?

SURVEYOR B: I must get myself a car.

SURVEYOR A: It's essential. Take her out and about. Impress her. Bring her to the Stars restaurant. She's dazzled — loses her head. Says to herself, "He's the one. He's showing me the big wide world."

(BABIS *brings another case, puts it on the steps and sits beside it.* YANNIS *is going inside.*)

BABIS: Have you got everything, Yanni?

YANNIS: We've nearly finished.

BABIS: Do you want me to help you?

YANNIS: There are only a few small things left.

BABIS: If *he* were here now, everything would be different.

YANNIS: Stelios?

BABIS: We wouldn't be like this. He'd have said a ... he'd have said the ... I don't know what he'd have said, but he'd have said something, and everything would have been different. He'd have made us think we were going somewhere better — with a joke — with lies even. Because he was a gambler, a dreamer, he would go along with things, and make them bearable. He took life as it came. Ah, Stelio.

YANNIS: Are you saving money again to leave?

BABIS: No. I don't know. I've lost my bearings. Did *you* never think of leaving?

YANNIS: I would never want to leave.

(BABIS *looks at him in surprise.*)

YANNIS: You don't believe it? No matter how much Australia, Brazil or America promised, no matter how much they impressed me, they'd never entice me away.

BABIS: Why?

YANNIS: I have my mother, my father. They're old now. If I went away and left them, and something awful happened, who would look after them?

BABIS: Yes, but this country has betrayed me — destroyed any faith I had in it. You work for three days, and then do nothing for the rest of the week. You can't even keep a roof over your head. You never know what's going to happen the next day. You're never secure in this country — anywhere! Everything is

THE COURTYARD OF WONDERS

taken from you as fast as you can get it. That's the way it is. It rained cats and dogs the whole night. The wind nearly took the roof off. And now look at the sun. As if it were May. Isn't it always the same? (*He goes off to the back.*)

(SURVEYOR A *comes in, and takes two rolls of plans off the steps.*)

SURVEYOR A (*to* YANNIS): I left the glass there. (*He points to it.*)

YANNIS: Thanks!

SURVEYOR A: Thank *you*!

(SURVEYOR A *goes off with the rolls. At the same moment, a* POSTMAN *comes into the courtyard, with a telegram in his hand. He reads the address aloud.*)

POSTMAN: Stilianos Yannopoulos. (*He glances around, and says it louder*): Stilianos Yannopoulos?

(YANNIS *looks as if he has turned to marble on the step.* ANNETO *comes halfway out of her loft.*)

POSTMAN: Yannopoulos. Does he live here or not?

YANNIS: At the back.

(The POSTMAN *goes to the back.* YANNIS *looks at* STRATOS *and* ANNETO.)

POSTMAN (*stands at the back and shouts*): Stilianos Yannopoulos. Telegram. (*Pause*) Is he out?

(BABIS *comes slowly out from the back.* STRATOS *goes into his room.*)

BABIS: What telegram?

POSTMAN: What do I know? Sign. Take it and read it.

BABIS: It's not for me!

POSTMAN: Oh well, in that case... (*He shouts*): Stilianos Yannopoulos. Telegram. Does he not live here? What am I supposed to do?

(OLGA *comes out from the back. She is dressed in black. She seems to be avoiding eye contact with the others.*)

OLGA (*to the* POSTMAN): Where do I sign?

POSTMAN (*confused by all the activity*): What? Ah, you. Here. (*He shows her with his pencil where to sign. He then gives her the pencil.*)

BABIS (*bursting out*): Leave it.

(OLGA *stands motionless.*)

70

ACT FOUR

BABIS: Don't touch it!
OLGA: Why?
BABIS: Did you hear what I said?
OLGA: Who'll take it?
BABIS: Nobody. Is he here? No! Stelios isn't here anymore, is he? So then, nobody has the right to take it. Nobody.
(VOULA, ASTA and MARIA *have come.*)
BABIS (*to the* POSTMAN): Bury it. Dig a hole and bury it. This whore mustn't get it.
POSTMAN: Why?
MARIA: He killed himself.
BABIS: *They* killed him!
POSTMAN (*to* OLGA): *You* are . . .
OLGA: I'm his . . .
BABIS: What are you? Don't say anything. Let his soul rest in peace. If *you* even think about him, he'll be turning in his grave.
OLGA: He was my husband.
BABIS: He was your husband, but *you* weren't his wife. You were his, in there. (*He points to* STRATOS's *apartment.*)
OLGA: Stop.
BABIS: Take *his* name and his telegrams — not Stelios's.
OLGA: Leave me alone.
BABIS: You're responsible for his death, do you hear? You!
OLGA: No!
BABIS: You and your lover made him fall into the quarry. You two, who thought he was worthless . . . a pimp, a fool. But he had more worth and dignity than the lot of you put together.
VOULA: Babi. Be quiet.
BABIS: Go away. Go away, all of you. Leave me alone. You all thought he didn't amount to anything . . . you never took him seriously. But I knew him. He told me everything. And I saw him crushed to pulp — lying in his own blood on the stones of the quarry. (*Emotionally*): Oh Stelio. Oh Stelio. (*To all of them*): Do you hear me? Oh Stelio. (*He goes and holds onto the wall of the terrace. His chest heaves as if it were about to burst.*) (MARIA *rushes to embrace* OLGA. *She kisses her, and strokes her hair. Her voice trembles as if she is in a feverish delirium.*)
MARIA: Don't. No. It's not your fault. I know, I know . . . my

girl... my Olga. We both had to... nobody knows... understands. You can ask *me*. Three years of loneliness. Having a husband and not having him. That's the worst. Olga... dearest.

(STRATOS *comes out to his door.*)

STRATOS (*decisively, and with suppressed anger*): Olga. Do you want to take the telegram? Take it if you want to. Don't listen to anybody.

(*They are all silent.* OLGA *remains undecided for a little. Then she goes to sign. Her hand won't obey her. She gives back the pencil. Amidst the general silence, she goes slowly out to the back.*)

POSTMAN: So... it's been returned! (*He writes something in his notebook, and goes out thoughtfully.*)

(STRATOS *goes into his apartment. A man's voice can be heard outside.*)

VOICE: Come, Mrs Maria.

MARIA: I'm coming. (*She comes into the middle of the courtyard, and looks around as if she were lost.*)

(*The voice outside can be heard again.*)

VOICE: We've loaded everything.

MARIA: Yes, I'm coming. (*To the others*): Goodbye again. Goodbye.

ALL: Goodbye. God bless.

MARIA: Where's Yoakim?

ASTA: He's outside... playing. (*She shouts*): Yoakim.

MARIA: Pity I won't see him. (*To* JORDAN): Mr Jordan. (*To all of them*): Goodbye.

ALL: Goodbye.

BABIS (*to* VOULA): Women... to hell with them. Go on in!

(VOULA *goes away to the back.* BABIS *comes and sits on the steps.* ASTA *approaches the terrace.*)

ASTA: It's not the first time we've been through this. We've had it three times worse. Why are you so upset about it, Jordan?

(YANNIS *goes to* BABIS. ASTA *goes to the back.* BABIS *has covered his face with his hands.* YANNIS *puts a friendly hand on* BABIS's *shoulder.*)

BABIS: I haven't the heart to try and emigrate again. For hours, I've

ACT FOUR

been wanting to go out on the street and scream. My old man was a soldier from 1910 to 1920. In the forties, I lost a brother, but that never stopped me following my orders to the letter. I always did whatever they told me. Why should I leave? Why should I go elsewhere? This is my country. I should be able to find everything I need here — work, bread, a house. I want them here ... here ... here!

YANNIS: *I* wanted to say that to you ... but I didn't know how you'd have taken it.

BABIS: What do you mean how would I have taken it? Is it our country or isn't it?

YANNIS: It's a fine country! But if everybody calls it useless, then spits at it and leaves, what'll happen to it?

BABIS: Can *anything* happen here?

YANNIS: It's not the worst. Isn't man about to reach the moon?

(*Pause. They look each other in the eye.*)

BABIS: I'm glad we'll be living near each other.

YANNIS: I'm glad too.

BABIS: Let's go and lend a hand, so's we can get finished. Otherwise the women'll take all evening over it.

(*As they go out to the back, they notice* JORDAN.)

YANNIS (*to* JORDAN): Babis and Voula will be neighbours again.

BABIS (*to* JORDAN): We'll get on fine, Mr Jordan, you'll see. Why are you so worried about leaving here? We'll be just as comfortable where we're going ... maybe even better.

YANNIS: Come on. Come down.

(JORDAN *stays silent.*)

BABIS (*to* YANNIS): We'll go and bring out the other things. When it's time to go, he'll come down. (*To* JORDAN): Won't you Mr Jordan? Of course you will!

(YANNIS *and* BABIS *go out to the back.* JORDAN *takes out a piece of cloth, and wipes his nose.* ANNETO *comes down from the loft with a large bag. It slips from her hand, and falls. As soon as she comes down, she lifts the bag hastily, and takes an icon out of it. She makes the sign of the cross, and kisses the icon. At the same moment,* OLGA *comes out from the back.* ANNETO *stuffs the icon into the bag.*)

ANNETO: Are you leaving?

OLGA: Yes, I'm off.
ANNETO: Your things?
OLGA: They'll come and get them.
ANNETO: Why didn't you call me to help you?
OLGA: There was no need.
ANNETO: If I had a daughter like you, I wouldn't want anything else. (*She falls on her knees in front of* OLGA, *and embraces her legs.*) I'm an old woman. I have nobody in the world. I never wanted it to be this way. (*She kisses* OLGA's *hands*): Nothing can be done about poor Stelios. Marry the other one. Don't be alone. Look at me. I'm so alone. He loves you very much. I know that. Every night . . . all night . . . even before the terrible thing happened . . . he'd walk back and forth lighting cigarettes . . . nothing else . . . just staying up all night smoking. (*She sees that* OLGA *does not reply. She kisses her on the cheek.*) You *know* he loves you. Take care of yourself. (*She goes to the back.*)

(STRATOS *takes one or two steps outside his door.* OLGA, *although she is not looking that way, is aware of him. For almost the whole scene, they avoid making eye contact with each other.*)
OLGA: Goodbye.
STRATOS: You're going?
OLGA: I'm going.
STRATOS: Goodbye then.
OLGA: Goodbye.
STRATOS: Do you want to . . .
OLGA: Don't.
STRATOS: I know. I think so too.
OLGA: Never!
STRATOS: Never! I know.
OLGA: It would make things worse.
STRATOS: They are already.
OLGA: Goodbye.
STRATOS: Olga . . . I loved you so much!
OLGA: Me too!
STRATOS: I want you to know that.
OLGA: And I want you to know it. (*She turns and looks at him.*

ACT FOUR

Then she makes her way towards the street.)
(*A* YOUNG MAN *comes in hastily. He goes towards* STRATOS, *looking cheerful.*)
YOUNG MAN (*to* STRATOS): Tell me, are they selling the door and window frames?
STRATOS: What?
YOUNG MAN: Are the frames for sale?
(STRATOS *turns away, and goes into his apartment.*)
YOUNG MAN: Why don't you speak to me? Am I asking you for money? (*He goes over to* JORDAN *and says to him*): Excuse me. I asked the other one, and he looked at me as if... strange people... they're obviously fed up talking. Tell me, please. Are the frames for sale? I see they're a bit the worse for wear, but the builder sent me to ask if they're available.
(JORDAN *stays silent.*)
YOUNG MAN: Are they?
(JORDAN *stays silent.*)
YOUNG MAN: They aren't? Why don't you say something? What have I said to...
(JORDAN *sees something outside. He half lies down, and holds on tightly to the edge of the terrace. The* YOUNG MAN *goes off bemused. The two surveyors come in with a* POLICEMAN. *They approach the terrace.*)
SURVEYOR A: Now then, old chap, will you come down? Come on now, and we can get on with our work. We want to leave our tools in, and board up the door. Work begins here tomorrow.
SURVEYOR B (*to* JORDAN): What kind of work do *you* do? Do you want to stay and help take out the rubble? (*To* SURVEYOR A): He could have ten drachmas a day.
SURVEYOR A: If he wants. Keep him for the foundations as well. (*To* JORDAN): What do you say, uncle? Are you good with a spade?
POLICEMAN: Why would *he* use a spade? The man *has* a job. He makes roof tiles. Don't you, Mr Jordan. Come down, and we'll all go and have a glass of wine together. The widow has opened a cask of the new stuff. What more can I do?
SURVEYOR A: It's my treat. Come on Mr... what's his name?
POLICEMAN: Mr Jordan!

SURVEYOR A: Mr Jordan . . . I see. I'll treat you to a litre of wine, and any appetisers you like. Are you . . .

SURVEYOR B (*to the* POLICEMAN): He won't listen to reason. Pull him down, or you'll force me to do it.

POLICEMAN: Please! Mr Jordan is a fine friend and neighbour. We told him to come down. He'll come down. Won't you? (*To* JORDAN): Tell me, where's your rifle? (*He laughs.*) That old bad habit of yours.

SURVEYOR A: Does he do target practice?

POLICEMAN: He can't stand cats. When he sees a cat — bam! The next door neighbours are always coming to the Station to complain. (*To* JORDAN): I . . . do you hear, Mr Jordan . . . I don't pay any attention to them. Come on down. Come down.

SURVEYOR A (*to* JORDAN): Look Mr, Mr . . . what's your name . . . what do you think you're doing?

(ASTA *comes in, followed by* ANNETO *and* VOULA. *They are looking agitated. They are followed by* YANNIS *and* BABIS, *who are laden with bundles.*)

ASTA: Come down Jordan, effendi. Why are you so grieved? They've even brought the police, don't you see?

VOULA: Don't hold on so tight, Mr Jordan. Your veins have swollen. You'll hurt yourself.

ASTA: Jordan, sweetheart. You'll have another terrace where we're going. There *is* one. I saw it with my own eyes. I'll cover it with rugs. I'll look after it for you.

YANNIS: Have pity on us. What have we done to you? Why do we have to beg you like this?

BABIS: Trust me, Mr Jordan. I swear on my mother's soul, I'll build you whatever you want with my own hands.

JORDAN: I don't want.

BABIS: I love you. My own father is dead. If he were alive, and asked me to fix him up a little nook, wouldn't I try my best? But he's not alive, so I'll do it for you. Isn't it the same thing?

JORDAN: They're throwing us out of here, Babi . . . they're throwing us out.

POLICEMAN (*going up to the terrace*): Don't be difficult. All these people here promising you the moon and the stars.

JORDAN: They're throwing us out again, Babi. They're throwing us

ACT FOUR

out. (*He holds on more tightly to the edge of the terrace.*)
POLICEMAN (*gently takes hold of* JORDAN, *and tries to pull him down*): We're offering you wine and food. It's shameful to have so many people begging you. And the girls are looking at you. (*He pulls him hard*): Come on now, before I lose patience with you!
(ASTA *kisses one of* JORDAN's *hands.* VOULA *goes to the other one. She caresses it, and tries to loosen it.*)
YANNIS: Leave him alone. He's my father. Get down from there. I forbid you. Babi!
POLICEMAN: I don't want to hurt him. (*He pulls at* JORDAN *with all his might, and breaks his hold.*) Come down.
(JORDAN *gives up all resistance. For a moment, he claws the air as if he wanted to strangle someone. At last, looking exhausted, he comes down from the terrace. The* POLICEMAN *also comes down.*)
POLICEMAN: That's it. Didn't I tell you . . . Mr Jordan's all right.
(JORDAN *goes and grasps the handles of the handcart.*)
BABIS: Leave it. I'll take the cart.
JORDAN: *I* will. *I* will, Babi.
BABIS: Come on. Let's go!
(*Everyone picks up their bundles and suitcases.*)
BABIS: Patience, Captain Jordan . . . patience . . . I'll fix up something nice for you — you'll see.
VOULA: What's come over me . . . I feel like singing.
ANNETO: God help us. You'd think we were going on a trip!
YANNIS: Babis and I have plans. Haven't we, Babi?
BABIS: We'll fix everything. On you go, Captain. Load up the vans. Everything'll be better, you'll see. Others have nearly reached the moon.
(JORDAN *pushes the cart.*)
ASTA: Holy Mother . . . we're finally leaving.
ANNETO: We're off.
(*Suddenly they all stand still.*)
BABIS: The best one is absent. There'd be a few laughs if he were still with us. Ah, Stelio. Come on then, Voula. What are you staring at?
VOULA: I'm coming.

ASTA: Yoakim . . . where is he? (*She shouts*): Yoakim. Yoakim. (*She goes towards the street, shouting his name.*)
BABIS (*to* YANNIS): Is that not heavy?
YANNIS (*elated*): Not at all! It's as light as a feather!
BABIS: Mine feels light too. (*To the women*): Come on. Go ahead. (*She shouts*): On you go Captain. Load the vans. Everything'll be better. You'll see. Others have nearly reached the moon.
(*They go out. Their voices, and the voice of* ASTA *calling for Yoakim, can still be heard for a short time on the street.*)
POLICEMAN: It's over. (*He shakes hands with the surveyors.*)
SURVEYOR A: Thank you very much.
POLICEMAN: It's my job. (*He goes out.*)
(STRATOS *comes out of his room with a case. He glances around the yard, and towards the back. He then goes out to the street.*)
SURVEYOR A: There were some strange people living in this yard.
SURVEYOR B (*making a dismissive sound*): Never mind about that. It's the same everywhere.
SURVEYOR A (*looking at his watch*): What came over the old man? Why didn't he want to come down from the terrace?
SURVEYOR B: Who knows?
SURVEYOR A: A quarter past two. I'm off.
SURVEYOR B: Right.
SURVEYOR A: Remember that chat we had about entertaining the ladies? Good hunting.
SURVEYOR B (*laughing*): Good hunting.
(SURVEYOR A *goes out.* SURVEYOR B *dawdles about the courtyard. He stands near the terrace, takes a good look at it, leans against the stairway and murmurs something that sounds like a school song.*)

LIGHTS OUT

—— THE END ——

THE FOUR LEGS

OF THE TABLE

FOREWORD

TO

THE FOUR LEGS OF THE TABLE

PRODUCED AT THE ARTS THEATRE, ATHENS, 1978

For the fifth time I am experiencing the great satisfaction of having a play of mine produced at the Arts Theatre and, as on previous occasions, under the direction of Karolos Koun.

By coincidence this year's production of my work in this theatre in the round is especially thrilling for me. Twenty years ago, on the same stage, *The Courtyard of Wonders* was performed, my first collaboration with the Arts, to which I owe so much. Often I hear people say to me, "Ah, that play continues to have the impact it had then . . ." On the one hand, as your playwright, I am flattered, but on the other hand, as an incurably ordinary Greek citizen, I think that if *The Courtyard* has not exhausted itself something has not gone well in our country. Whether true or not, the fact is that I continue persistently to cover the same ground with the same mechanisms which stimulated me when I first began to write — almost thirty years ago now. All my plays are simply episodes of one and the same story. But how could it be otherwise? It seems that the receiver which sometime in our youth pieces together the optical and the emotional determines our position in life. It resembles an unsuspecting self-constructed personal (ancestral) fault line which remains with us to the end.

Thanks to a second coincidence, this year's play has yet another relationship, a thematic one, with *The Courtyard*. The group of people, who under a common fate, clash in *The Four Legs of the Table* is, as a social force, the very opposite of the world in *The Courtyard*, and to a great extent is responsible for its wretchedness. *The Courtyard* reflected the tragic consequences for the poor which had their source in the Second World War and the Civil War, and the shameless favouritism involved in the reconstruction of the country. The present play reflects the consequences of those same times and events, but this time for the ruling social class — their great economic advantages and, with those, the stabilisation of their socio-political power.

THE FOUR LEGS OF THE TABLE : FOREWORD

In *The Four Legs of the Table* I come to grips with this power — or, more precisely, I toy with it. Who are these "fellow-countrymen" who think they have the monopoly on God's grace and have yoked the fate of our country and all of us to their personal interests?

Yet the play is not as bombastic as the commentary I'm making on it. And its story is a very simple and common one in 1978, which is the year of this play. The seven siblings, women and men, inheritors of a great manufacturing business, live under the tyrannical immortality of a father with nine lives who, although in a permanent vegetative state, holds 51% of the shares, thus keeping his heirs in ignorance of the future position each of them will have in the firm. Ruthless scheming and fierce rows become constant among them, as they struggle for the position of leadership in the firm. In the fiercest of their disputes, in which they engage, by every means at their disposal, in internecine war, they discover, to their despair, that they are chasing after something that is irrelevant: they are investing in a future which they cannot control. The problem of their positions in the firm turns into anguish at their position more generally. They become reconciled. They are friends again. They look backwards instead of forwards. They eulogise the hitherto objectionable immortality of the father, and the eldest utters the tragi-comic remark: "We may no longer have children but we still have papa."

I hope that with these words — for the writer it is always difficult to explain certain things — I am helping you to enter more quickly, and better prepared, into the world of the play.

I thank Karolos Koun and his colleagues, visible and invisible, involved in the performance, who with such love — which means endless hours of work — have given flesh, bones, and voice to my play.

IAKOVOS KAMBANELLIS

THE FOUR LEGS OF THE TABLE

A play in two acts and three scenes. There are two scenes in Act One. Act Two consists of a single scene.

THE CHARACTERS IN THE PLAY

PAPA (ASIMAKIS KAVALAS) ninety-nine-year-old founder of the family business

KOSTAS KAVALAS — eldest son of Asimakis

TONY
GEORGE — other sons of Asimakis
MANOS

ALICE
IRENE — daughters of Asimakis
MARY

AUNT (VASO) — sister of Asimakis

A NURSE

In the dialogue the vocative forms of some of the male character's names occur : Asimaki, Kosta, Mano.

A NOTE ON THE PRONUNCIATION OF NAMES

Personal and place names (and the name of a dance) in the text of the play where the position of the stress may not be obvious.

Asimakis	A-si-**ma**-kis
Amalia	A-ma-**li**-a
Amalitsa	A-ma-**lit**-sa
Averofides	A-ve-**ro**-fi-des (*d* as *th* in *other*)
Birbili	Bir-**bi**-li
Boubouki	Bou-**bou**-ki
Chrisoula	Chri-**sou**-la
Euridice	Eu-**ri**-di-ce (English pronunciation)
Irene	two syllables as in English (or I-**ri**-ni as in Greek)
Kalamata	Ka-la-**ma**-ta
Kalliopi	Kal-li-**o**-pi
Kavalas	Ka-va-**las**
Kostas	**Kos**-tas
Manos	**Ma**-nos
Markos	**Mar**-kos
Melissourgou	Me-lis-sour-**gou**
Metaxas	Me-ta-**xas**
Mykonos	**My**-ko-nos
Patisia	Pa-**ti**-si-*a*
Singri	Sin-**gri**
Theofilos	The-**o**-fi-los
Thodoros	**Tho**-do-ros (*d* as *th* in *other*)
Tripoli	**Tri**-po-li
Tsaldaris	Tsal-**da**-ris (*d* as *th* in *other*)
tsamikos	**tsa**-mi-kos
Vaso	**Va**-so
Vangelis	Van-**ge**-lis
Velonis	Ve-**lo**-nis
Venizelos	Ve-ni-**ze**-los
Veryina	Ver-**yi**-na
Zappeï	Zap-**pe**-i

ACT ONE
SCENE ONE

A spacious room, very sparsely furnished but at the same time giving the impression of a rich household.

At back, on the left, a nurse sits knitting rhythmically; she has obviously been doing this for hours on end. At the right, on the wall, are two or three Byzantine icons.

In the middle of the room, on a bed, lies the ninety-nine year old founder of the Kavalas business empire, Asimakis Kavalas. It is difficult to make out whether he is alive or dead.

On the left, front of stage, are a low table and two small gold lacquered chairs, upholstered in expensive material.

The eldest son KOSTAS, *about sixty years old, enters with his sister* ALICE *who is some years younger.* ALICE *looks around for her bedridden father, and then sweeps down on him, deeply moved.*

ALICE: Papaaa . . .
KOSTAS: Calm down *please.*
ALICE: I can't bear it, I can't . . .
KOSTAS: If you can't bear it, let's go!
ALICE: Don't be angry with me when I'm so upset.
KOSTAS: You promised to behave yourself.
ALICE: It's breaking my heart.
KOSTAS: Look dear, if you *really* can't stand it, let's go.
ALICE: No, I won't go. I want to see my papa. You have no right to prevent me seeing him.
KOSTAS: You're upsetting him with your shouting. Can't you see?
ALICE: *You're* making me shout.
KOSTAS: Don't get me angry on top of everything else!
ALICE: How much longer will I be able to see him? Has that not occurred to you?
KOSTAS: It's my fault for letting you come here in the first place!
ALICE: What do you mean *letting* me? Does he belong to you only? Whatever rights you have, I have too, and George and Tony and Manos and Mary and Irene! Are we not all his children?
KOSTAS: Give me strength! Wasn't I the one who said, "Come and see him?" How dare you say that I'm preventing you!
ALICE: So you're doing me a favour letting me see papa? That's it,

you feel you're granting me a favour?
KOSTAS: Will you pull yourself together and speak more quietly? Otherwise you'll have to calm down outside and *then* we can talk.
ALICE: *You* should pull yourself together and calm down, not *me*!
KOSTAS (*pointing to his head*): Are you feeling all right?
ALICE: Your behaviour is unbelievable. You have him here all the time, inaccessible and forbidden. We must have your permission to see him . . . to see whom? Papa. Our own papa. (*She weeps.*)
KOSTAS: Spare me the waterworks!
ALICE (*after a short fit of crying*): It's over. I'm sorry.
KOSTAS: I'm going out of my mind.
ALICE: Don't misunderstand me. Put yourself in my position.
KOSTAS: All right. Forget it.
ALICE: I got carried away, I know.
KOSTAS: You weren't carried away. You were led on. *They* led you on!
ALICE: I don't like to accuse other people.
KOSTAS: Of course, but how much longer do I have to hear that I'm Cerberus keeping the doors closed to you all — for how long?
ALICE: You said we should forget it.
KOSTAS: I'm not talking about you my dear. I'm talking about the others. At least you have the honesty to admit your mistakes.
ALICE: I'm really very sorry.
KOSTAS: All right. It's over.
ALICE: May I stay a little longer?
KOSTAS: As long as you like, only don't upset him! I told you from the start he hears and understands everything! It would be terrible for him to think we were mourning him while he's still alive.
ALICE: I wouldn't want that.
KOSTAS: I know, but I had to warn you. If he is still hanging on, it's because he's got this fighting spirit! Physically, he's exhausted. If we break his morale, it'll be as if we've killed him!
ALICE: God forbid!
KOSTAS: The doctors made it clear to me that at this stage whatever organs are not paralysed become particularly sensitive. (*He points to his ears*): It isn't important that he can't react! But it is absolutely certain that he hears and understands better than ever. He is completely lucid.

ACT ONE : SCENE ONE

ALICE (*approaching the bed*): Darling papa!
KOSTAS: The mind of an athlete — the body of an invalid.
ALICE: How long has he been like this?
KOSTAS: Almost ten years.
ALICE: I mean how long since the last attack?
KOSTAS: Aaaah... hmmm... Tuesday afternoon. And he was fine you know, fine. He could swallow a little cream and a little juice. He was moving his hands and opening his eyes now and again.
ALICE: Did he speak to you at all?
KOSTAS: Of course... well... you couldn't understand what he was saying... a few incoherent sounds... but anyway he was trying to make himself understood.
ALICE: Kosta, I'm worried.
KOSTAS: What else can I tell you? The doctors believe that with no complications he will make a complete recovery.
ALICE: May God hear them.
KOSTAS: Amen! In any case Alice, I'm very optimistic.
ALICE: Why exactly? What are you counting on?
KOSTAS: On his past, his history.
ALICE: Yes, but is it not more serious than last year?
KOSTAS: No comparison! Last year's crisis was much worse.
ALICE: But last year we had given up all hope.
KOSTAS: Not last year, the year before. The crisis the year before last was more serious than last year's.
ALICE: Now I remember. The doctors had given him up.
KOSTAS: You're confusing everything, Alice. It was three years ago that they told us they couldn't promise anything.
ALICE: But of course, and he asked for communion.
KOSTAS: No — he asked for communion five years ago. I remember it clearly because a year before, when he had the serious attack, six years ago that is, it was the same day as his birthday. He was exactly ninety-three years old!
ALICE: That was when we had definitely written him off. You're right.
KOSTAS: You're wrong. Seven years ago, we wrote him off when his pulse dropped to thirty.
ALICE: So it's the seventh crisis?
KOSTAS: The ninth. There were two before that. *You* were in America then, or was it Sweden?
ALICE: Sweden.

THE FOUR LEGS OF THE TABLE

KOSTAS: Well anyway, we thought that was it, but he came back from the dead — literally.

ALICE: So Kosta, as time goes on he gets better and better?

KOSTAS (*after looking her in the eyes*): In one sense. If you believe that after each crisis he comes back healthier than before, then of course that's up to you! (*Suddenly he goes over to his father, listens to his breathing, comes back to* ALICE *and takes her by the hand*): Come, sit down.

(KOSTAS *and* ALICE *sit.*)

KOSTAS: Alice, as you can well see, papa is able to ride these crises now. I thought that for the time being I wouldn't bother asking any of you to come — you know — one from London, one from Zurich, the other from Iraklion etc. etc. This whole gathering is pointless, but it's better this way than you all accusing me of monopolising papa and his crises, and even his death, God forbid!

ALICE: But Kosta, I . . .

KOSTAS: I'm not referring to anyone in particular! But generally siblings and in-laws see conspiracies and plots. Since you've never been married, you may have remained an innocent — an honest soul — but don't forget the things you accused me of a moment ago!

ALICE: I didn't mean them, I swear to you.

KOSTAS: But someone else put those ideas in your head.

ALICE: Perhaps.

KOSTAS: And I know who! In any case, may I remind you of what I said ten years ago with all of you present? That I could not tolerate our putting father into the Annunciation Hospital! That I would rather convert my house into a hospital than have him far away from his family — as if he hadn't seven children. And it was made clear by everybody that you didn't think this was right, because I would be able to manipulate him at your expense! I would persuade him to change his will the way I saw fit. You all went as far as that — not to see that I am performing a duty towards him, because we owe him everything, but to suspect that I'm doing it to exploit him, to fleece our dying father so as to rob the rest of you.

ALICE: It's shameful, I admit . . .

KOSTAS: Let me finish — and who were all these suspicions aimed at? At me, who, if I had wished, could have immediately taken the lion's share, just as I could take it now if I wanted. But I

88

ACT ONE : SCENE ONE

won't do that because I'm not selfish. I'm not blinded by my own interest. I see further. I am interested in the whole!

ALICE: But you are the eldest. If you don't take charge, we have no head of the family.

KOSTAS: It's not simply that we'll have no head of the family. We'll be ruined! But nobody else considers this. They're each waiting for papa to die so's they can grab their share and set up their own business! But if this happens, we are all destroyed! If we go our separate ways, our dominance in the marketplace will be permanently wiped out!

ALICE: You mustn't allow that! Nobody has the right to destroy papa's work, not even his own children.

KOSTAS: That's why I do everything to make him live! And I've vowed that he'll never die — at least, as long as I live there will be no question of father dying, I assure you! It's the secret of the sphinx that holds us together! What will happen when the will is opened? Have you thought about that?

ALICE: Oh, my God, what you've just said . . .

KOSTAS: Everybody will want their own slice of the pie!

ALICE: Kosta . . . what does it say in the will? Do you know?

KOSTAS: No, of course not! But I suspect that it isn't what it should be. If it doesn't maintain our strength, it will sow the seeds of our ruin! He wanted to be fair to all of us, but didn't consider what chaos he'd be throwing us into! It seems that when you have one foot in the grave, you forget what you've achieved. You're interested only in what people think of you after your death. You don't care about leaving a world where order asserts itself by consuming others!

ALICE: Kosta, this'll sound stupid . . .

KOSTAS: Go on, dear . . .

ALICE: Can the will not be amended?

KOSTAS: What did you say? (*He goes to his father again and comes back to* ALICE): That's a bit sly, isn't it?

ALICE: Can it not be amended?

KOSTAS: And supposing it *can* be, then what?

ALICE: You must do it!

KOSTAS: That's my predicament. I can and yet I can't. I'm on the horns of a dilemma! On the one hand, I have a duty to keep us all in one piece, and on the other I can't deceive anyone.

ALICE: You wouldn't be deceiving anyone! You know very well they've already taken more than their share, without doing as much as you.

KOSTAS: I know, but they are vultures — selfish, greedy and power-mad! Thankfully, you're not like them. You had the good luck not to marry and have children. You didn't become a crook to secure their future. But the others . . .

ALICE: What are we to do?

KOSTAS: I can be as tough as need be, but in this case I'm alone, completely alone! And it is a moral decision that I cannot be burdened with alone! I must draft another will and somehow make him sign it!

ALICE: Is he able to sign?

KOSTAS: He will be able. The solicitor will even agree with whatever I want and whatever I say! It's not the technical side of things that concerns me, it's the moral question. It's my misfortune to be a thinker, and a thinker doesn't easily escape doubt. On the other hand, he can be influenced when not utterly alone.

ALICE: You are not alone.

KOSTAS: I am, Alice.

ALICE: You're not anymore!

KOSTAS: What do you mean? Look me in the eye!

ALICE: I would give my life not to have papa's work destroyed.

KOSTAS: Dear Alice, what you say is to your credit, and I'm very touched — but you must realise that you'll be undertaking a great responsibility with me.

ALICE: I do realise and I'm not afraid.

KOSTAS: Then I'm going to show you something. I'll open a secret door for you that only I have the key to.

ALICE: What do you mean?

KOSTAS: Do you want to talk to papa? Do you want him to understand what you say, to open his eyes and see you?

ALICE (*with emotion and gratitude*): Oh, Kosta . . .

KOSTAS: Quietly . . .

ALICE: But you said he hadn't any strength.

KOSTAS: Sshh! For me he has, and from today he will have for you as well. You and I will be the only ones who'll communicate with papa!

ALICE: And do you think he'll recognise me?

KOSTAS: Do you swear that none of the others will know about this?

ALICE: On my life.

KOSTAS: Wait until I get him ready.

ACT ONE : SCENE ONE

ALICE: Darling papa!
KOSTAS (*to the* NURSE): Sister, come here please. (*To* ALICE): Only my wife and the nurse know what is about to happen, and no-one else. (*To the* NURSE): Let's raise him up a bit.
NURSE: Of course.
(*The* NURSE *and* KOSTAS *together raise the old man on the pillow. He continues to appear lifeless.*)
KOSTAS: Where did you put the newspaper and his glasses?
NURSE: I have them here.
(*The* NURSE *takes them out of a bag and gives them to him.*)
KOSTAS: Thank you sister. Thank you very much. You may go now.
(*The* NURSE *goes out.* ALICE, *who is very curious, tries to see which newspaper* KOSTAS *is holding. He shows her.*)
KOSTAS: The Financial News! Come over here.
(KOSTAS *indicates the foot of the bed. Then he puts the glasses on his motionless father. So that he can smell the newspaper first,* KOSTAS *brushes it against the old man's nose.*)
KOSTAS: Papa! Your paper! Papa, can you hear me? Your paper — smell it. They've brought your paper. Come, that's good, smell it! Good — smell it again. Take the first breath. Breathe, papa! Go on. Again — and again. Come papa. Good — that's it. That's the way.
ALICE: He's coming to!
KOSTAS: Sshh. Now touch it, papa. (*He rubs the newspaper against the old man's right hand*): Touch it. Open your fingers. Can you hear me papa? Touch it. It's your paper. Can you feel it? Open your fingers. Take it. Hold it. It's yours. Good, hold it tight. It's your favourite paper. It has good news today. That's it papa, that's it. Your other hand too. Good. Hold it with both hands. Hold it tight now. Good, papa. And now your eyes — your eyes papa! We've put on your glasses. Now you must open your eyes! Your eyes, papa.
ALICE: He has opened them.
(*The old man becomes more and more animated as he takes notice of the newspaper. The "corpse" begins to come to life.*)
KOSTAS: We're doing well at the Stock Exchange, you see? We bought another forty-five shares yesterday and seventy on Monday. That's one hundred and fifteen before the end of the week! The National Shares have gone up, but the Greek ones are doing better. Aluminium shares have taken a leap. Etemé and

Violan have fallen, but cement shares are stable.
(*The old man reacts with gurgling sounds.*)
KOSTAS: Look how well the Spinning Mills are doing. (*To* ALICE): Speak to him.
ALICE: Papa.
KOSTAS: It even says they're issuing new shares.
(*The old man gurgles.*)
KOSTAS: Yes, yes, we'll have to see about that too, eh?
ALICE: It's Alice papa, your little Alice.
KOSTAS: I've sounded the bank, and in principle they have no objection, nor will the finance committee, as long as it's a question of long term investment.
(*Gurgles from the old man.*)
KOSTAS: What's that papa?
ALICE: Have you eaten your nice little dinner?
KOSTAS: What are you saying papa? We'll have fifteen thousand for the price of five? Which? The franc? The mark?
(*The old man gurgles.*)
KOSTAS: What do you mean papa? I don't understand . . . aaah, the dollar? No, it doesn't affect us at all. Don't worry. The pound bothered us . . .
ALICE: Talk to him about me . . .
KOSTAS: . . . but luckily it has stabilised. (*To* ALICE): Stand behind the paper . . . (*To the old man*): and our Alice is here. Can you see her papa? Smile at our Alice, *your* Alice. Now the pound is stable and doesn't affect exports. Look at the bastards — look at them — on their knees! The idiots are heading for the junk yard.
(*The gurgles become more animated than before.*)
KOSTAS: You've wiped the losers out. They thought they could take you on. (*He laughs.*) Look here, they've fallen by 850. (*He bursts out laughing.*) They're falling by a hundred shares every week.
(KOSTAS *can't control his laughter. The old man, exhausted, lets the paper fall, closes his eyes, and reverts to semi-consciousness.*)
ALICE: Dear God!
KOSTAS: It's nothing.
ALICE: What's wrong with him?
KOSTAS: Absolutely nothing. He's fine.
ALICE: Why did he collapse like that again?
KOSTAS: He saw what he wanted to see. What else would he do?

ACT ONE : SCENE ONE

(*He gathers up the newspaper.*)

ALICE: Are you sure?

KOSTAS: This happens every day when we're reading our paper. Isn't that so papa? (*He takes off the glasses and caresses the old man's head*): Tomorrow, lionheart. Rest now.

(KOSTAS *draws* ALICE *aside.*)

ALICE (*not taking her eyes away from her father*): How long will he stay like this?

KOSTAS: Until tomorrow, when he reads his paper again! He doesn't wake up even to eat! What you saw happens only when he follows the stock market.

ALICE: What a remarkable man!

KOSTAS: A great man! There's no way I'm going to let him die before it's certain who will succeed him! Before he can prevent a huge empire from crumbling into dust. If there are problems, we'll find a solution. I'll have to supervise the making of a new will! You saw with your own eyes that I can make him sign. I only have to want it.

ALICE: You *must* want it. You can't give up now.

KOSTAS: You're right. (*He embraces her*): Thank you. Without you I wouldn't have had the strength to decide.

ALICE: And don't dither.

KOSTAS: As quickly as possible.

(*The* NURSE *enters.*)

NURSE: Excuse me.

KOSTAS: What is it?

NURSE: They're waiting for you in the lounge.

KOSTAS: How many have come?

NURSE: All of them.

KOSTAS: Good. Tell them we're on our way, sister.

(*The* NURSE *goes out.*)

KOSTAS: "Once more unto the breach . . ." Come Alice. Let's go.

ALICE: Have the others seen papa?

KOSTAS: They all saw him yesterday. Of course they didn't see what you saw. Let's go.

ALICE: Isn't he like a sleeping lion?

KOSTAS: Yes, but he needs another to keep watch.

LIGHTS OUT AND SCENE CHANGE

ACT ONE
SCENE TWO

A drawing room in the same house. The other five siblings are there — TONY, MARY, GEORGE, MANOS *and* IRENE.

At the beginning, and for a short time, we see and hear them in a half-light. Their cries make them sound like various birds of prey, and therefore symbolise their personalities.

ALICE *and* KOSTAS *enter. Normal lighting resumes.*

KOSTAS: Welcome everyone!
(*The brothers and sisters greet one another cordially, embracing and kissing.*)
KOSTAS: It's so long since we've been together like this.
TONY: It's all rather difficult.
MARY: Very difficult.
IRENE: Maybe so, but we *are* brothers and sisters.
GEORGE (*sarcastic*): Seven. Long may we live. Ha ha ha . . .
ALICE: Well I for one am never tired of seeing you all.
KOSTAS: Sit down. Don't stand about.
MARY (*to* ALICE): Did you see papa?
ALICE: I did. Isn't he amazing?
KOSTAS: Mano, why are you hiding in the corner? Come here.
MANOS: Where am I supposed to sit? I'm fine as I am.
TONY: Aren't we going to stop this idle chit chat and say something more to the point?
KOSTAS: I propose . . . listen to me . . . I propose that before we begin the discussion, you should hear a real surprise! I found it by chance in father's desk. Have you all got something to drink . . . Mary?
MARY: I'm fine.
(KOSTAS *takes some papers out of his pocket.*)
KOSTAS: Bring your drinks over, and make yourselves comfortable. Alice, will you read it to us please?
ALICE: Me?
KOSTAS: Come on, you read so nicely.
GEORGE: Did you know that the old man fancied himself as a poet? Ha ha ha . . .
ALICE: How could we forget? He used to make me recite his work.
"There I was up in the sheepfold,

ACT ONE : SCENE TWO

Together with the shepherds . . ."
TONY: Don't go on. What *is* this?
(*He points to the manuscript that* ALICE *is holding.*)
KOSTAS: It's a short autobiography which means a lot more.
IRENE: Get on with it Alice — read.
ALICE: All right. What beautiful handwriting. Look, and he left school when he was only ten.
GEORGE: Don't start blubbing, or we'll be here all night.
ALICE: Do you see me crying?
GEORGE: She's about to.
MARY: Give over. Are you going to read the thing, or shall I read it myself?
ALICE: Easy dear. Are you all in such a hurry?
TONY: No, but we didn't come here to mess about!
ALICE: Well, I'll begin.

My name is Asimakis Kavalas. My father was Constantine and my mother was Amalia Melissourgou. I was born in 1877, and I have a younger sister called Vaso. With the little education that I have, I am able to set down my history for my children, grandchildren, great-grandchildren and great-great-grandchildren to read and learn how I established our company, took it to the top and reigned supreme in the market. I give my blessing to whoever respects and develops what I have created, and I curse whoever harms it. I advise you to stick together and work together like the fingers on a hand, so that no-one will ever be able to take the throne from you. When I was seven years old, and my late mother was pregnant with the girl, an evil man stabbed my father over a dispute about land. Although I was only a child, I swore vengeance, but God, who always stood by me, did that for me. A mule kicked the murderer in the chest, and killed him instantly. My widowed mother took her brother's advice and sold the land. With the money, they went into partnership in a grocer's shop. As soon as I was ten years old, she took me away from school and put me to work in the shop. It seems that I got my financial genius from God; I quickly fathomed the mysteries of the trade. At the age of eighteen, I was managing the shop, but I didn't get on well with my uncle because of his backward ideas! We began to disagree — he took his share and opened another shop, determined to put me out of business. But before two years were over, I had wiped him out and he was begging me to have pity on him. How could anyone else try to destroy me? As well as the retail, I had started up a wholesale business. I would buy oil at half-price from the villages, and there came a time when I was sending more than 20,000 okas of oil to Piraeus. The year the olive crop failed throughout the Peloponnese, I had, in my warehouse, 32,000 okas which I sold at two and a half times the normal price. Then I started dealing in the dried fruit harvest, and I made the farmers buy all their groceries and clothes at my shop, otherwise I wouldn't buy their produce.

At the age of thirty, I had the biggest shop and warehouse in Argos and on top of that 30,000 in cash which I loaned with interest. I worked day and night, and didn't spend a farthing on fine clothes and entertainment. My one joy was to go to a festival to hear the unforgettable Thodoros Bey playing my favourite song on the clarinet: "Speak to me Birbili." I loved dancing to it. Another pleasure was to hear stories of how great wealthy families such as the Zappeï, the Averofides, the Singri and other Croesuses had made their fortunes. I dreamed that one day I would be like them. Obviously, I was much sought after as a husband. God gave me Chrisoula, the daughter of Mark Velonis from Tripoli. We had seven fine children and lived in harmony until God took her to him.

Since, through my marriage, I had acquired a large dowry, and since there were no more opportunities for me to expand my business in Argos, I decided to open a shop in Athens. I bought a large property in Hermes Street, near the church of the Holy Angels. There were storerooms at the back of the building and a yard with a number of sheds. There was a large apartment above the shop.

By good fortune, the previous occupier, who made ouzo, had left some distilling equipment in the back storerooms. When I got the regular business into shape, I took on men who knew how to manufacture the drink. I printed advertisements showing a man wearing a kilt, with an Italian prima donna drinking our ouzo, which I distributed around the shops. Even before it was available, everybody was saying: "Where is this ouzo so that we can all try it?" The result? When the business took off, we couldn't keep up with the bottling. Now pay attention to the important part of the story. We did well with the ouzo, but others manufactured it too. Unfortunately, I didn't have the monopoly on it. Then God put a dream in my head. It was as if I

ACT ONE : SCENE TWO

had gone to Constantinople to give a cask of ouzo to the Sultan as a present. They took me to the Sultan's Palace, and as soon as he saw me, he raised his gilded sword and shouted: "Listen infidel, if you don't make golden ouzo for me, I'll behead you!" I said: "You mean brandy, my lord?" "Brandy, infidel, brandy!" I woke up in terror, but when I came to my senses, I fell on my knees and thanked God. I had been inspired. By the following day, I had already begun to plan my new venture — very discreetly — so that the secret wouldn't leak out. I reckoned that only the French knew how to make brandy, and I immediately wrote to an acquaintance of mine who had been working as a tailor in Paris since he was a child. I asked him to find and send me an expert. I would pay him whatever he wanted. Within two months a Frenchman, Louis Dupois, arrived but he was no good. I provided him with whatever wines and materials he wanted. For a year, he carried out experiments, but pigs would have flown before any brandy would've appeared. Once, he said to me: "Give me my share and I'll go home — I can't do it." "You're not going anywhere," I told him. "I'll kill you first, and then the Sultan will kill *me*." I set to work alongside him. We concocted a mixture, and whatever happened, we hit on an excellent drink. Others might say it was a fluke, but I say it was God's will. I had found a gold mine and anyone could call it what they liked. Anyway, I began production and bottling, with a gold label printed in Italy. This happened when King Constantine was in conflict with Prime Minister Venizelos. The king became seriously ill through the shameful behaviour of that scheming Cretan. The people kept a vigil outside the palace. They brought the icon of the Holy Mother from Tinos, but illness is illness. I loaded up a horse trap with bottles, went to the palace and handed them to the crowd, saying: "Drink to the health of Constantine and to the death of Venizelos." The response, needless to say, was very enthusiastic. A courtier came out to see what was happening, and I gave him some bottles to take inside! Whoever believes in God and the king is carried on the wings of luck. Within one week, on a Tuesday, near midday, a royal carriage stopped in front of the shop. They had come to buy fifty bottles for the royal family. And what do I hear on top of that? The ailing Constantine had drunk five glasses of brandy at one go, and from that moment had begun to recover. The news spread like wildfire, and Constantine could hardly refuse to buy a few bottles. I was allowed the title: "By special appointment to His Majesty the King", and I received a medal. The bank gave me a loan to build a large factory. So, I got into the fast lane and nothing could stand in my way. Even the 1922 Asia Minor disaster benefitted me, because, until then, I had competition in Smyrna.

In addition, I hired some commercial travellers, refugees from Smyrna who were multilingual and would work for almost nothing. I picked out the best and sent them abroad. They opened up an export trade for me with Egypt, Syria, the Lebanon, Persia, Turkey, Romania, Bulgaria, Spain, Morocco and Abyssinia.

Greece revived under the Metaxas dictatorship, and King George proposed that I become an M.P. But I said to him: "Your Majesty, I can help the throne much better as an economic force than as a minister." He understood exactly what I meant. I got another loan and built a second and then a third factory, expanding production to all kinds of alcohol — wines, liqueurs, even champagne. Then came the Second World War and the Occupation. I didn't bother any German and no German bothered *me*, so when it was all over I was again in control. I would buy up small wine-making concerns, and close them to get them out of my way. The King came back again and showered me with medals and honours. Every government took notice of me. After all, politicians may be elected by the people, but they are appointed by us. And just as the people should not be governed with kid gloves, but with an iron fist, so the politicians need a firm hand, otherwise they get above themselves.

You who will inherit from me must keep your eyes open. Work hard, use your brains, have faith in God and the King and whoever represents them. Never say, "This is enough." You must keep on developing, because only in this way will you be strong and always able to destroy the competition. Through my prayers, my fatherly love and the wisdom of Almighty God, may you learn from my example that if you continue to be worthy, you will rule the market until the end of time.

ALICE: Poor papa.
GEORGE: What a testimony.
MANOS: When did he write this?
KOSTAS: It must have been ten, fifteen years ago.

ACT ONE : SCENE TWO

MANOS: And why are you disclosing it to us now?
KOSTAS: I found it recently. What are you driving at? I don't understand.
MANOS: Nothing.
IRENE: What do you intend to do with this?
KOSTAS: Nothing. We have read it as he wished us to, and now we'll keep it. It's a real family heirloom.
IRENE: Yes, but will you keep it as it is . . . ?
TONY: Of course. What do you mean?
IRENE: Shouldn't we amend it? He writes things that people will laugh at if they hear them. He makes us all out to be hicks, while everyone believes we are a family with a military history.
MARY: Rubbish.
IRENE (*dismissively*): "Speak to me Birbili" — a peasant song!
GEORGE: And what was the 1821 Revolution if it wasn't (*sings*) "Speak to my Birbili . . ."
IRENE: He served in a grocer's shop. I don't know — I find that all very unseemly.
TONY: I think there's one point that needs to be amended or omitted — where he says some incompetent started making the brandy, and it came out right entirely by chance. That proves that papa and all of us are swindlers!
KOSTAS: But there's no question of publishing any of this. These things belong to history, to our family history. In my opinion, the value of this testimony lies in the mandate he has left us!
MANOS: Each to his own opinion.
KOSTAS: I beg your pardon?
MANOS: For God's sake, does it not annoy you all that we come out of this looking like peasants?
MARY: Am I likely to lose sleep over that? I'm interested in what *I* am — not in what papa was. When all's said and done, we all started the same way. But tell me, have we come here to gossip about the past or to discuss something more practical?
TONY: I absolutely agree that we should change the subject. We have other, more important things to talk about. Kosta . . .
KOSTAS: As you wish. Anyhow, I have a duty to keep you informed about this, as I have about everything else, so . . .
TONY: That's enough. Let's get on with it.
GEORGE: I'm having another. (*He goes with his glass to the drinks tray.*)
KOSTAS: I must state exactly what the situation is. Papa has

suffered another stroke. Happily, this was even milder than the previous ones, and so not only has his condition remained stable, it even shows some improvement. In any case, the doctors who are treating him assure me that even without any improvement, papa has many years ahead of him. (*Choking with emotion*): I'm sorry, but like you I'm overcome with joy and pride that this man is my father. And I believe that it is a gift . . .

(*Suddenly* AUNT VASO, *papa's very old sister, enters in her wheelchair.*)

AUNT: Ah, here you are. I thought you were in your study.

KOSTAS (*hurriedly goes to take her off stage*): Don't interrupt us, Aunt. Don't interrupt us.

AUNT: But I want you. Where is Man . . . Kos . . . Ton . . .

KOSTAS (*pushing her out*): Excuse us, dear Aunt, not now.

ALICE: Poor Auntie!

GEORGE: She'll bury us all . . . ha ha ha . . .

KOSTAS: As I was saying . . . Aunt Vaso — truly the living history of our family! . . . As I was saying then, it's a divine gift that father's state of health remains as it is, and will continue to do so! Firstly, because he is our father and secondly because not one of us can know what consequences his absence would have, both for the family and for the firm.

MANOS: But he isn't in the firm any more.

KOSTAS: Actively he isn't, but in spirit he is — as long as fifty-one percent of the shares are kept in his name.

MANOS: After all . . .

TONY: Wait, slow down. I might have something to say, but it seems *I* have to wait.

MARY: I think we all have!

KOSTAS: Of course I invited you for a discussion.

TONY: Go on.

KOSTAS: From one point of view, it seems irrational that we should want this uncertainty to drag on — he *will* die — he *won't* die — an uncertainty that affects decision-making as far as the business goes. Production and sales remain static! Not one of us undertakes any initiatives, because we're always playing the waiting game. But I think that papa's longevity seems set to persist. He has come through nine strokes. We must get used to this, deny that it is a transitory state, and see it as permanent!

MANOS: But what's going on here? Have we come here to be lectured?

ACT ONE : SCENE TWO

ALICE: What's your problem?
KOSTAS (*to* MANOS): Did you hear what I said?
MANOS: Am I deaf?
KOSTAS: I don't think I was referring to the ancient tomb at Veryina; it was father I was talking about.
MANOS: I'm off... first father's autobiography, now a whole lecture. What did we come here for? A literary afternoon?
TONY: Mano, sit down. Sit down when you're told. I'm speaking to you. *Listen* to me, will you?
KOSTAS: He's been nervous lately, our little Manos.
MARY: Now that you mention it, I'm getting bored too. Is your speech finished, or is there more?
IRENE: You are all impossible!
MARY: Enough of the airs and graces. You've yawned forty times.
IRENE: Don't be impertinent.
(AUNT VASO *comes in again.*)
AUNT: I want Alice. Is Alice here? Where is...?
GEORGE: We missed you.
KOSTAS: Aunt, please, we have business to discuss.
AUNT: Listen, Alice dear...
KOSTAS: I'm not Alice, I'm Kostas.
(*He wheels her out.*)
TONY: Why doesn't he tell them to keep her inside?
ALICE: It's a pity to see her like this.
KOSTAS (*comes back in, trying to control his irritation*): I've said all that had to be said. I want to finish by making an appeal to you all as a brother, with all the responsibility that being the eldest brings. Thanks to his strength and endurance, father's longevity will continue! As a consequence, inasmuch as we are not only siblings but at the same time inheritors of a business empire, we must conduct our relationships in the light of what I have just said. I want to be the first to declare that since family unity must be preserved, as well as the integrity of the firm, I will make any sacrifice necessary at the expense of *my* personal interests.
ALICE: I agree, and we should all follow your example.
(KOSTAS *goes to get a drink.*)
MANOS: May I also make a statement before we go any further?
GEORGE: Why do you butt in all the time?
TONY: Why are *you* bothered?

KOSTAS: Feel free. I never prevent anyone from having their say, especially when I am the host.

MANOS: Well then, let me say that I'm no longer going to play the role of the family idiot. (*To* KOSTAS): You know very well how much I contribute to the firm, and that for understandable reasons we don't disclose this — do we? Whenever you employ my special methods, you can't begin to express gratitude for what you call my invaluable counsel! You have said again and again that without my extreme measures, we wouldn't be standing so firmly on our feet!

KOSTAS: Perhaps...

MANOS: No perhaps about it. Do you want me to tell you when? The day, the hour? But as soon as the crisis is over, you shove me aside again. Well, if you think I've decided to vanish into thin air simply because I have to take certain covert measures on your behalf, you are very much mistaken. On top of that, you know I'm always unjustly treated. So, I may as well inform you that I've decided to lay claim to my rights in full, and by any means necessary!

KOSTAS: Dear little brother, each of us is where papa has put us! If you are unjustly treated, which I very much doubt, *I* haven't wronged you!

TONY (*to* MANOS): You know very well that I'm not satisfied either, but we're not talking about what happened in the past!

MANOS: I was talking about the future as well.

TONY: Hold it right there!

KOSTAS: I beg your pardon, but I was also talking about the future.

TONY: Yes, but not quite in the same way. You were talking about how we should conduct our relationships with one another. We are thinking about father's will.

KOSTAS: The will can be taken for granted! It was drawn up by a solicitor many years ago. And a will, as you all know very well, is sacred and inviolate!

MARY: We shall see when the time comes.

KOSTAS: What do you mean, Mary — that if you don't like it you'll contest it?

MARY: That, and a few other things!

KOSTAS: Have you lost your wits?

MARY: Who can vouch for how this will was written? Who can guarantee that he wasn't influenced, that he didn't do what

ACT ONE : SCENE TWO

others told him? How can we be sure that *they* won't make him invalidate the old will and sign a new one?
KOSTAS: You never did hesitate to come out with wild accusations.
MARY: Happily.
ALICE: What kind of way is this to behave? Why are you interfering? Remember that you're only a woman.
MARY: And because I'm a woman I have fewer rights?
ALICE: Let's leave the men to deal with things. These are questions for men to discuss.
MARY: Financial matters don't concern men *and* women! I see I'll have to defend my own rights.
IRENE (*hysterically*): This is dreadful!
MARY: Stop acting so disgusted — like a superior being! If you can't stand us, have a stroll around the shops and see what the heels are like on this season's shoes!
IRENE: Shut up! Do you hear me? I said shut up!
TONY: I'll put both of you out if you don't stop this.
GEORGE: Let them carry on. It reminds me of the old days.
MARY: She gets on my nerves. We're having a serious discussion, and Madam over there finds us dreadful!
MANOS: So let her give up her rights and leave us in peace!
IRENE: Very clever!
MARY: Give up her rights? Which of us spends as much as Madam over there? Three people — and they have seven cars and three houses here, as well as the ones in Switzerland, New York and London. If you want to get hold of her, she'll be either in Bermuda or the Bahamas! Give up her rights, when all that she has isn't enough!
IRENE: I'm not even going to dignify that with an answer. This is the behaviour of the streets!
TONY: Have you finished? You've taken the discussion down to gutter level.
MARY: I can't stand hypocrisy.
TONY: I don't mind what language you use, as long as we don't become abusive. (*To* KOSTAS): May I have the floor?
KOSTAS: But I'm not presiding.
TONY: You said before that we should see our relationships in a new light.
KOSTAS: It's necessary because ...
TONY: Personally, I have no objection, but I want the doctors to assure me that papa's condition is in fact what you say it is!

KOSTAS: You dispute this?
TONY: No, but I'm concerned about the lack of further proof.
MARY: So am I.
KOSTAS: But any one of you who wishes can consult these doctors. Do you want me to arrange a meeting for tomorrow?
ALICE: Why not? We could all stay and have dinner.
KOSTAS: Good idea.
TONY: Excuse me, but perhaps I haven't made myself clear. I mean that other doctors should examine him, not those who are attending him!
MANOS: I absolutely agree.
KOSTAS: Are you serious? It's your right of course, although I could see it as not just offensive, but also . . . I don't know . . .
TONY: I have no intention of offending you! I may be a bit cold and pragmatic yes, but offensive, no. Even if it becomes necessary for us to have recourse to the law — something that I do not wish to happen — you will never hear the slightest insult from my lips!
KOSTAS (*stupefied*): The law?
GEORGE: What's happened to Aunt?
TONY: I said, if necessary.
KOSTAS: Why, is there a circumstance that makes it necessary?
TONY: It was mere conjecture!
GEORGE (*to* KOSTAS): Will you permit me?
KOSTAS: Very serious conjecture!
TONY: If it offends you, that's your problem.
GEORGE: May I?
KOSTAS: Did I say that it was my problem?
TONY: I did, and if it worries you, find out the reason and don't throw the blame on me.
GEORGE: Will you let me say something before I lose my mind?
TONY: Go on, speak.
GEORGE: You've been talking so much, but I don't understand a word you're saying! Speak plainly so that we can all understand — stop the riddles.
TONY: What's he saying?
KOSTAS: That he doesn't understand what we're saying.
GEORGE: Up to where you said that papa has seven lives, I understood everything. From then on, I haven't a clue. I'm sharp enough, but not to the point where I can understand what *you're* saying!

ACT ONE : SCENE TWO

IRENE (*hysterically*): It's like a jungle in here! A jungle! I can't listen to this anymore!
ALICE: My head is splitting!
MANOS: I suggest that somebody take control.
MARY: And that minutes should be kept.
KOSTAS: Ask for whatever you want. How will the minutes be kept? Is this a family gathering or a shareholders' meeting?
TONY: Why have we changed the subject? I requested that papa should be examined by reliable doctors. Those who agree with my proposal, raise their hand.
(MARY, MANOS, IRENE *and* GEORGE *raise their hands.*)
Five votes for, two against.
KOSTAS: I withdraw. Finish the discussion as you wish. Do whatever you like!
TONY: If you leave, you're simply making your position worse!
KOSTAS: What did you say?
TONY: After all, will my proposal change anything?
KOSTAS: Everything!
TONY: Why? Will the doctors that we appoint contradict the others?
KOSTAS: I haven't the slightest doubt that they will come to exactly the same conclusion!
TONY: Then what's bothering you?
KOSTAS: This appalling lack of faith in me! This atmosphere of suspicion and distrust!
TONY: And who is to blame for all this?
KOSTAS: So you admit that you came here predisposed — ready to dispute my integrity!
TONY: Sorry.
MARY: Never mind "sorry". Why "sorry"? We've come through a lot to be able to speak out at last. Why retreat into politeness and hypocrisy again?
KOSTAS: Are you all in agreement?
ALICE (*to* TONY *and his supporters*): I didn't know what your intention was.
GEORGE (*to* KOSTAS): Listen, please. We are brothers and sisters, and I think it's good that we're open with one another, because if your brother doesn't tell you the truth, who will? Your enemy? So, for somebody who likes order and few words, the situation for me is like this: We get the impression that you are intending to take everything from us!

THE FOUR LEGS OF THE TABLE

KOSTAS: You bastards!
TONY: Please . . .
MANOS (*to all of them*): Stand firm!
ALICE: My God.
MARY: I'll sue you.
IRENE: Where's my handbag?
 (AUNT VASO *comes back*.)
AUNT (*to all of them*): Before you go I want you to do something.
KOSTAS: I *told* you Aunt, I'll bring you in before we leave.
AUNT: But by then I'll forget what I want.
KOSTAS: Tell me what it is, and I'll remind you.
AUNT: Where is my little Irene?
IRENE: Here I am, Aunt.
AUNT: Listen, Alice dear.
IRENE: Is it Alice you want or me?
AUNT: And who are you?
IRENE: Irene.
AUNT: They washed my hair today. What's it like? Is it nice?
IRENE: It's gorgeous.
AUNT: Mary.
MARY: Yes, Aunt.
AUNT: How is Vangelis? Is he any better?
MARY: Better? Vangelis?
KOSTAS: Tell her he's getting better!
MARY: What's all this?
KOSTAS: We haven't told her!
AUNT: Don't forget to kiss him from me, the rascal!
GEORGE: Ha ha! Dear Aunt Vaso. How could we ever forget *you*!
AUNT: Bend down. I'm tired looking up. Tell your mother-in-law I'm very cross that she never sets foot in here to see me.
GEORGE: She doesn't come?
AUNT: It's been years.
GEORGE: But it's been years since . . .
KOSTAS: Sshh! We haven't told her.
AUNT: I don't get out or I would see her myself! Has your father-in-law come back from Egypt?
GEORGE (*to* TONY): Have *you* got a father-in-law in Egypt? Your turn.
TONY: How's it going, Aunt?
AUNT: Is he still in Egypt?
TONY: He stayed there.

ACT ONE : SCENE TWO

KOSTAS: We haven't told her.
TONY: Unbelievable!
AUNT: It was the same with your uncle Anthony. He went to America and didn't come back.
GEORGE: It's her condition.
AUNT: I want you to do me a favour, Kosta. Are you there? (*To* GEORGE): Tony, are you listening to me?
GEORGE: I'm listening.
AUNT (*to* MARY): Alice, listen.
MARY: Yes, Aunt.
AUNT: Irene dear, I want you to bring all of them someday — uncle Anthony, Vangelis, Theofilos, Euridice, Kalliopi, your father-in-law and your mother-in-law, all of them, and we'll have a party like we used to!
MANOS: A party — or the Second Coming.
TONY: You haven't told her about any of them?
KOSTAS: I think Aunt's tired. I must take her in.
AUNT: No, I'm not a bit tired. Let me stay here. They torment me all the time. They don't even let me watch television!
KOSTAS: So as not to tire you.
AUNT: Where is my little Alice that the prince baptised?
ALICE: Dear Auntie — here I am.
AUNT: Do you see this envelope? I want you to take it to the palace. Will you ask for Mrs Boubouki and tell her love from your Aunt Vaso, and that you want to see Queen Frederica. I have a cheque here for the orphans. Tell her I'm sorry I can't come myself because of my rheumatism.
ALICE: Don't worry Auntie. I'll tell her exactly as you say.
AUNT: If she isn't there, don't leave the cheque, because they would steal the Holy Mother's eyes in that place. Put it into her hands only, and tell her that I pray for the health of herself and her children, and that I have rheumatism.
ALICE: I understand Auntie. Come now and I'll take you to your room.
AUNT: Let Alice take me.
ALICE: I *am* Alice.

(*She wheels her out while* AUNT *blows kisses to the others.*)

MANOS: And where will you send this cheque now?
TONY: That's a good one. You've told her nothing.
KOSTAS: What point is there in telling her?

GEORGE: The living history of our family. (*He bursts out laughing.*)
MARY: What a bizarre situation.
KOSTAS: But what do you want me to do? Sit down and teach her about political developments over the last decade?
MARY: I'm not talking about politics. Shouldn't she have been told that all the people she mentions have died?
KOSTAS: Why should we upset her at her age?
MANOS: That's bloody nonsense. You don't tell her anything because that's the way you work. That's your character! You like to cast a fog over everything to assert your dominance!
KOSTAS: He's crazy!
MANOS: But we've put an end to that. Today we have made our decisions.
KOSTAS: Get out of my house!
MANOS: Papa will be moved to Tony's house!
KOSTAS: What?
MARY: We all have faith in Tony!
KOSTAS: I agreed that your doctors should examine him but not . . .
TONY: Why should it annoy you that I take him? Am I not his son too?
KOSTAS: Look, my patience has been stretched to the limit!
MARY: And ours!
TONY: He will be moved tomorrow morning. This is what most of us want, so you can't oppose it. Understand?
KOSTAS: Don't even think about it.
TONY: When I talked about a lawsuit, I was being hypothetical at first. Don't push your luck.
KOSTAS: Aaah . . . (*He clutches his chest and begins to stagger.*)
ALICE: Help . . .
(ALICE *runs to him.* KOSTAS *falls into a chair.*)
IRENE: A little water.
GEORGE: Loosen his tie.
ALICE: Animals!
MARY (*to* ALICE): Old maid!
ALICE (*to* MARY): And you're nothing but a merry widow!
IRENE: We're all hicks!
MANOS: How perceptive of you!
(KOSTAS *drinks the water that* IRENE *brings him.*)
KOSTAS: Thank you. It's over. It was nothing. Allow me to withdraw. As for everything else, do as you see fit. I can only

ACT ONE : SCENE TWO

    say, "Father forgive them, for they know not what they do."
    (KOSTAS *departs accompanied by* ALICE.)
TONY: It wasn't easy for me to treat him so roughly, but he has completely lost my trust. He's dug his own grave. (*To all of them*): Will you always trust me to take care of papa?
ALL: Always.
TONY: May I appoint the doctors I consider suitable?
MANOS: You have complete freedom.
ALL: Agreed.
TONY: I swear on my children's life I won't betray your trust.

LIGHTS OUT

ACT TWO

A large room, like a sitting room, in Tony Kavalas's house. TONY *stands near the bed-ridden old man, observing him and listening to him. He then takes a cassette player off the table, brings a chair and sits near the old man. He presses the "play" button, and we hear the folk song "Speak to me Birbili" played on the clarinet. He watches closely to see if the old man is reacting, but nothing happens. He puts the cassette player against the old man's ear and again watches for any flicker of expression on his mask-like face. Disappointed, he turns off the cassette player, sighs loudly, rises, puts it on the table, carries the chair back to its place, and then walks up and down thoughtfully. He stops and gazes at his father.*

TONY: You've become a problem, papa — a big problem. In fact, I'm beginning to wonder if you're doing this on purpose. Either you're holding on deliberately, or you're pretending to be alive and yet not alive. We don't know what's happening to us, so we can't make any decisions! But between ourselves, you always perplexed us. It was your policy. Whenever you realised that one of your sons was about to make a stand, to be worth something, to take any initiative whatsoever, you would start to complain that we were going through difficult times, and we should leave our big ideas for the future. But let's not kid ourselves, sir. You fabricated those difficult times. I know of two strikes — I'm not so sure about the third — which, if you had wanted, could very well not have happened! But you provoked them, so that you could turn to me and say: "You idiot. We have strikes on, and you're looking for a position of authority." Do you hear what you make me remember? God forgive me! But look here, you sly old fox . . . you're breathing regularly, your heart's ticking like a clock, you eat, you drink, your needs can be attended to with the precision of a timetable — and the one thing you won't condescend to do is open your eyes and say a word. Am I wrong? You're oppressing us with this silence of yours. Don't you realise that? You continue to be just as oppressive now as you have been throughout your life. You'll never change. What are you waiting for? You're ninety-nine years old. When will you grow up? I don't know what illusions are making you rest

ACT TWO

on your laurels, but as regards your children you ought to be ashamed. As a father you are a failure. You didn't let us develop any of our personalities. We've grown old without having created a single thing. What did we do with our lives, I ask you? You liked to call us your heirs and successors! We were your fetchers and carriers, not your successors! We were like slaves! And since you've ceased to create anything, we haven't even been *that* important. We're undertakers, pallbearers. We carry around a dying legacy. I don't mean that you're dead, that you've no life in you. I'm being metaphorical. You understand what I mean, you shrewd old man. God forgive me. (*He hears a noise in the background*): Who is it?

(TONY *moves to go off the stage, but stops when he sees* MARY *coming in. She is carrying a beautifully wrapped parcel.*)

TONY: Come in. I was expecting you.

MARY: I've brought him a lovely knitted jacket. Where shall I put it?

TONY: Leave it aside for the moment until the others arrive, so's it's not too obvious that you got here first.

MARY: How is he today?

TONY: See for yourself. I don't want to give you the wrong idea.

(MARY *leaves the parcel to one side, then approaches her father and looks closely at him.*)

MARY: He seems worse to me.

TONY: And to me too.

MARY: His colour is bad. Are you sure nothing untoward has happened?

TONY: I don't think so.

MARY (*bending low over her father and listening*): You're right. His breathing is regular. Did the doctor see him?

TONY: Of course.

MARY: What did he say?

TONY: Same as always, neither better nor worse. But there's one thing I can't understand. Where did our little brother Kostas get the idea about father's health improving all the time? How come he saw it and I didn't?

MARY: We'll do what has to be done. Never mind about Kostas!

TONY: I don't mean that from the day I took on papa he *hasn't* been improving! Didn't you say his colour is bad? What if Kostas sees it, and says anything to that whining little creep Alice? Whatever way you look at it, it's to our advantage that father should appear healthier in my hands than in his. It would be preferable if his colour were better, seeing as we're all gathered here for his nameday!

MARY: Shall we put a bit of colour on him?

TONY: What?

MARY: We're not doing anything bad! If there were a medicine that could do the job, would we not give it to him? (*She takes her make-up out of her bag.*)

TONY: I would never have thought of that.

MARY: That's because you don't use make-up. You don't fight every day in front of the mirror to repair the damage.

TONY (*with a stifled laugh*): You're incredible.

(MARY *has begun to put make-up on her father, while* TONY, *who is watching with great interest, begins to speak.*)

TONY: Mary, I fear we may be implicating ourselves. Almost every day, I sit here and watch him for hours. I have given the nurse instructions to take note if he speaks or moves — nothing. Not the faintest glimmer! He's in this permanent state of lethargy. Put a touch on his lips.

MARY: Good idea. They're very pale.

TONY: The thought has just struck me. If he's been like this for two months in my hands, he must have been the same when Kostas had him! Either we've been wrongly accusing Kostas of keeping papa in order to influence him, or he discovered some way of bringing him round and having him in his power.

MARY: Nothing would surprise me.

TONY: Nor me — but how?

MARY: He might have got his hands on a drug of some kind. There are simulants available that would raise the dead. Look, I wouldn't put it past that unscrupulous, deceitful man to resort to any means of grabbing the lion's share! Have you found a completely trustworthy doctor? Could you ask him what the best stimulant is? If you haven't, let me handle it; I can get hold of the pills.

TONY: It mustn't be pills; he can't swallow pills. It must be in drops or by injection. I've already asked my own doctor. Don't ask any other. There's no need.

MARY: And he said that there *is* such a drug?

TONY: There is. It's German.

MARY: Can it be found in Greece, or should I pop over to Germany and get it? I can easily go. It's no problem. My son is studying

ACT TWO

there. No-one will wonder why I've gone.
TONY: When can you go?
MARY: Whenever I like — tomorrow even.
TONY: Better the day after tomorrow! Good, that's *very* good.
MARY (*having finished putting make-up on the old man*): How does he look?
TONY: No question about it — a huge difference. You want improvement Mr Kostas? You've got it.
(MARY *puts the make-up back in her bag.*)
TONY: You must bear something in mind, by the way. The doctor does not recommend that we soak him in stimulants! It would affect the heart, and cause palpitations that he might not be able to endure.
MARY: This man? He's as strong as an ox!
TONY: I'm only telling you what the doctor said.
MARY: Papa has defied the prognosis. I say we do whatever *we* think is best, and leave the doctor to his theories.
TONY: What happens if we accidently kill him? We must think of everything, you know.
MARY: He has survived so many crises. Will a mere stimulant hurt him?
TONY: He has survived, but how can we be a hundred per cent sure?
MARY: We can't. Who can be sure that he'll be alive tomorrow? How do I know that the plane I get into won't explode in the air? And how do you know *you* won't suffer a heart attack at any moment? Listen Tony, there's no other solution: we have to make him sign the new will. We either give him the stimulant or play fairy-godmothers.
TONY: You're absolutely right. Here, let's have a cigarette. (*He offers her a cigarette.*)
MARY: Listen Tony. Do you want us to be honest with each other?
TONY: I don't think there have ever been any secrets between us.
MARY: I don't know what you feel at the bottom of your heart, but I'm not happy that papa's still alive, in this state! I'm not saying I'd be glad, but I wouldn't be sorry either if he died. What relation has this corpse to our papa? Just because the body's still functioning, does that mean papa is really alive? As far as I'm concerned, he died on the day he ceased to know what was happening to him. And if you must know, I'm disgusted when I hear you all talking about his immortal soul! What soul? He

looked after his own interests, and we should do likewise. Why pretend we're happy that he's still alive, simply because we're incapable of agreeing what to do afterwards. As soon as we all come to an agreement, we will finally understand the harm he's done to us by not dying when he should have. Instead of looking to the future, we're worried about whether the past is getting better or worse!

TONY: Don't be so callous!

MARY: Why? Because I call a spade a spade? It doesn't matter, as long as there's one in the family who isn't a liar. And please, stop playing these games with me.

TONY: Games? What games?

MARY: Every time we're together, you always play the same trick. You irritate me, and I begin to say things *you* should've said. You force me to grab the snake out of the pit. And so, you have a clear conscience because *you* didn't say anything bad. (*Pointing to papa*): He has four sons, not one of them a real man.

TONY: If I admit that I totally agree with everything you've said, will you be satisfied? What does it matter who calls a spade a spade, or who only thinks it? When all's said and done, you're more open and I'm more inward-looking. It isn't that we're not men!

MARY: Yes, but if we don't say these things, how will we come to an understanding? By telepathy? Enough of the nonsense.

TONY: All right, don't get excited! Do you think we should confide in the others about the stimulant and all that?

MARY: We'll have to think about it.

TONY: Could you rely on that idiot Irene for example? Once, during a holiday in Mykonos, she hired a servant just to keep the flies out of her room. She thinks that whatever she has is hers by the grace of God.

MARY: Well no, I'm not as crazy as to trust that fool!

TONY: I should think not! What about George? Why would you trust *him*? He is good. He is brilliant, but if he gets nervous he's capable of blowing everything sky high! A few years back, if you remember, he came to blows with the deputy governor of the bank — over the merest trifle — which resulted in our credit being reduced for a whole year. It's bad enough that when he gets drunk he doesn't even know what he's saying!

MARY: *I'm* afraid he'll object to everything. He's very emotional. So it's only Manos we can . . .

ACT TWO

TONY: No way . . . that's completely out of the question!
MARY: You mean Manos?
TONY: He's the most dangerous! He, my dear, has a sick mind. He's worse than his wife, so they're well matched! We've filled the factories with retired village policemen to keep an eye on the staff. He has a file on every employee, and dismisses people for the slightest thing! I'm tough, but he's depraved! He's a pathological fascist! Not for ideological reasons, but because he's a lunatic! If he weren't rich and from a good family, he'd be a thug! Can you trust a man who is constantly paranoid, who doesn't have one friend, who doesn't enjoy life? I'm surprised they even have children!
MARY: The two of them are very aloof and unfriendly — just like their mother.
TONY: Deep down he hates *us*, just as he hates everybody.
MARY: Yes, but he's the only one who would agree about the stimulant and whatever else . . .
TONY: Because he is evil. He has a black soul! And he hates papa! Mary, we're not doing this out of malice. We're doing it because we think it right! Manos would do it because he is evil! Just remember, if we involve him, he'll accuse us one day of killing father and of extorting his signature. He will accuse us, blackmail us, and be in the driving seat for good! That man dreams of one thing only — to get rid of us all, and come out on top. He was useful as far as overthrowing Kostas was concerned. Now, we must rid ourselves of *him* as quietly as possible, like they do with hitmen when they're no longer useful.
MARY: Don't go on. You've convinced me . . . so we're the only two left!
TONY: Does that bother you?
MARY: It annoys me that the two of us will do everything and the others will benefit without having risked a thing.
TONY: That's what I want to discuss. I am a practical person. I don't believe in this romantic notion that the will should provide equal shares for all of us.
MARY: I agree! But in the name of equality, we decided to push Kostas out of the way!
TONY: We did that when he was playing the leader. Personally, I've never believed much in equality. The only thing that concerns me is not being made a fool of. If Kostas is clever, *I* am more so! But apart from getting rid of him, we're not doing

well. Papa is not dying, and the eldest successor is useless. He has no courage. The future looks bleak for us.

MARY: Tony, we haven't much time. I mean, what decision are we going to reach?

TONY: Mary, I see a will which basically favours the most capable person, so that there's one strong hand guiding the company's fortunes.

MARY: And if the will favours you, then how do I fit into all this?

TONY: You won't be doing it for nothing. You'll secure a good share in advance, and whatever else is available.

MARY: Give me something to drink. I'm a bit keyed up. I'm not made of iron, you know.

TONY (*cheerfully*): Whisky?

MARY: What else? (*She goes over to her father*): Oh papa, what are you doing to us? All hell will break loose the day your will is finally opened — if we can call it *your* will!

TONY: We'll celebrate afterwards! And anyway papa... (*going over to the old man*): ... didn't you always say, "Blessed are the keepers"? — isn't that what you liked to say?

MARY: They'll blame you papa. You'll hear things after your death that you've never heard in your life. They want equal shares!

TONY: Papa, are they stupid or what? How can anyone talk about equal shares and equality and all that nonsense? While you were in control, did *you* believe in equality? What's happening? Have we suddenly become upper-middle-class Marxists? In that case, we must formulate a new political theory — communism for the wealthy capitalist. All industrialists and businessmen must form a collective. We'll have a capitalist-communist system at the top, and everybody else at the bottom. Ha, we don't give a shit for their equalities, do we papa?

MARY: Tony, someone has come.

TONY (*listens*): Wait! (*He goes out for a moment and comes back.*) Kostas and Alice are here!

(TONY *goes out again.* MARY *puts down the glass she is holding, and picks up the parcel as though she has just arrived.* ALICE *and* KOSTAS *enter with* TONY *behind them. They are both holding parcels.*)

ALICE (*kissing* MARY): Happy birthday to papa. May he live long.

MARY: Many happy returns to him.

KOSTAS: Hello Mary. Let's celebrate for him.

MARY: And next year too.

ACT TWO

ALICE (*goes over to papa and kisses him on the forehead*): Many happy returns, dear papa.

KOSTAS (*goes over and caresses papa's hair*): Eh papa, many happy returns. May you live to be as old as the hills.

ALICE: Thank God he looks so well, eh Kosta?

KOSTAS: Ah yes, extremely well! And why wouldn't he? Does Tony not do as much as I did?

ALICE (*to* TONY): He was most unfair.

KOSTAS: Alice *please*! That's all in the past! Don't listen to her Tony. I assure you that I am happy with the way things are. What has the doctor said to you?

TONY: Same as before. (*He laughs.*) Condition stable — no change.

KOSTAS: Good, good.

ALICE: How is Aunt?

TONY: If you mean her famous complaint, she's not well. She has to be looked after constantly, day and night.

KOSTAS: I know, I know.

ALICE: Poor Aunt who was so kind and helpful — to have become so useless. It's heart-breaking.

TONY (*to* KOSTAS): I hope you feel good about loading her onto me.

KOSTAS: Aaah. Since you stubbornly insisted on having papa, you must have Aunt as well. They're a package deal.

(KOSTAS *and* TONY *laugh.*)

ALICE: I brought him a little present. Where shall I put it?

TONY: Give it to me.

KOSTAS: And I have something.

TONY: Mary, bring yours over too. I think we should arrange them nicely on the table. (*He places the gifts on a small table near the bed*): You'll be asking what point there is — he can't enjoy them after all.

ALICE: It doesn't matter. You mean well, and that's the main thing.

KOSTAS: In any case, life is full of illusions. What harm is there in one more?

TONY (*turning towards the back of the stage*): Excuse me, someone has come. (*He goes out.*)

KOSTAS: Mary, what's your son doing?

MARY: He's still in Dusseldorf. Perhaps I'll fly over to see him the day after tomorrow.

KOSTAS: Is he continuing his postgraduate studies?

MARY: Of course. He's doing very well, I must say. Since he wants to learn as much as he can, let him learn! Some people have said to me, "How much longer will he be studying?" Is he annoying anyone — are *they* paying? Let him do what he wants. *I'm* paying.

KOSTAS: It's up to you, of course.

MARY: And *your* son, where is he now?

KOSTAS: He's here now.

MARY: Ha, we haven't seen him at all.

KOSTAS: He *is* here.

MARY: Won't Amalitsa be giving birth any time now?

KOSTAS: Next month.

MARY: The third little grandchild!

KOSTAS: I'm a real grandfather now. (*He laughs*): You're making me feel my age!

MARY: Won't you get yourself something to drink?

KOSTAS: Later. I'm not much of a drinker myself.

ALICE: Well, I want one.

MARY: Come and I'll pour you a stiff one. You'll be the lush and soul of the party.

ALICE: You're not far behind.

(*As the two women go towards the drinks table,* KOSTAS *goes over to papa and examines him. He notices a strange scent, and suspects that something is not quite right.* IRENE, GEORGE *and* MANOS *come in, along with* TONY. *The three also have gifts for papa.*)

GEORGE: Everybody here? Good! Well then, in the first place, many happy returns to our monster on his nameday. Secondly, it's a good thing that we've started to get at one another's throats in such an open way. It means that we don't have to see one another too often. Ha ha! We've had so many quarrels that one forgets how the other is doing. Now, we'll wear ourselves out kissing and saying, "How are you?" "Very well thanks, and you?" That old peace and love scene is in pieces now, and the only way family unity can be achieved is with, "I'll fleece you, you'll fleece me, we'll fleece him."

(GEORGE *laughs heartily. The others, except* MANOS, *pretend that they can take his joke.*)

GEORGE (*to* MANOS): Why shouldn't we laugh? Are we at a funeral? We're having a party. I really like family gatherings. I've a soft spot for the family. Haven't I papa? (*He goes over to papa and kisses him noisily*): Why should I wish you many

ACT TWO

happy returns? You have no need for such wishes — adding to the years is a hobby for you. Are we putting the presents here? Yes — here's the aftershave you like.
(GEORGE *leaves his gift on the table.* IRENE *and* MANOS *do the same, but don't bother much with papa.*)

TONY: I'll go and bring Aunt in for a while to get it over with. They almost have to keep her in there by force.
(TONY *goes out.*)

GEORGE: Bring Aunt in. Bring her in. Aunt is the soul of the house. (*Going towards the drinks*): Mano, what will you have? What can I get for you?

MANOS: Would you be so kind as not to concern yourself on my account.

GEORGE: How can I not concern myself? You look like you're about to be executed!

IRENE: Now stop it, both of you.

MANOS: If the purpose of this gathering is to listen to his jokes, then you should've warned me not to come.

GEORGE: What's stopping you enjoying yourself? Will output levels fall? Excuse me, but I don't tell jokes — I philosophise in a joking manner. If I were an ancient Greek, I'd be a Diogenes for all *you* know. (*He raises his glass*): Your good health.

MANOS: Shall we leave papa here or take him to his room?

KOSTAS: I don't know. It isn't my house. I'm not interfering.

MANOS: Oh, by the way — I have some rather unpleasant news. The minimum wage increase has been determined — and women's wages are now on an equal parity with men's.

KOSTAS: Are you sure?

MANOS: They phoned me from parliament.

KOSTAS (*loudly*): Where will it end? What do they think this country is — Sweden?

MANOS: Our wonderful democratic government!

MARY: What's going on?

MANOS: They're raising the workers' standard of living to whet their appetites for further endless demands.

MARY: Have they been given their increases yet?

MANOS: Indeed they have.

GEORGE: How can you blame the government? If they didn't give increases, there'd be more strikes!

MANOS: We could have a lock-out and let them die of hunger. This plague can't be cured by half measures.

ALICE: Honestly, I just don't understand this. We can see that wage increases make the worker greedy, and yet the government keeps giving in.

KOSTAS: The government doesn't pay the increases — *we* pay them. They carry out this policy at the expense of others.

MARY: Swindlers!

KOSTAS: The workers should have been given no concession from the start. It's a shame papa can't speak, otherwise he would have a few things to say on the matter. When the working man felt grateful for his rewards, he was reasonable and loyal; you could communicate with him! From the day they introduced protective legislation and such, the working man started to believe that we're stealing from him. Gratitude turned into strikes, blackmail and greed. And some people like to call *this* progress.

MANOS (*to* GEORGE): If you think that's ridiculous, listen to this. They're attacking us on all sides. Manual workers on the one, white collar workers on the other. And the vine-growers are ready to put up their prices. A bunch of criminals who have infiltrated the unions are stirring them up. Until now, we determined the price of the grape, and now they're fixing it. It wouldn't annoy me if they were doing it to earn another crust, but they do it because they hate us. These days nobody goes hungry, so they can't use bread as an excuse for their class struggle. They are driven simply by hate. They hate us, I hate them — so we're quits!

IRENE: Enough of the politics. You're beginning to bore us.

ALICE: Worse still, you're depressing us.

MARY (*to* IRENE): What does it matter, as long as you get some idea of the trouble we have earning a living.

IRENE: It doesn't interest me. Here in Greece you talk politics all the time — is it any wonder you're always in a mess? They never discuss politics abroad, so they have peace and quiet.

GEORGE: We all have a good laugh, though.

MANOS: How nice it was when you weren't speaking.

KOSTAS: In any case, let's not simplify matters. Damn it, the government *must* understand that this isn't Sweden! The Greek worker will have the same rights as the Swedish worker in two hundred years or so! Let him learn to be patient!

(TONY *comes in bringing* AUNT *who has make-up on today. She is dressed formally, even wearing a hat.*)

TONY: Excuse us for being so long, but Aunt wasn't ready.

ACT TWO

AUNT (*angrily*): Is she going to tell me what I'm to wear? Bring me my hats, or I'll call the police.

ALICE: Good evening, Auntie.

AUNT: Was anybody speaking to you? (*to* TONY): Bring me to him. Why have you left me here?

(TONY *brings her close to her brother.*)

AUNT: Asimaki. What's he doing? Is he asleep?

TONY: He's tired.

AUNT: Isn't he the one? He sees fit to sleep when we've come to say happy birthday. He was jumping around all morning, and I said to him, "Be patient until this evening", and now he's fallen asleep. Well anyway, he'll wake up. After a good sleep, he'll be as right as rain.

TONY: And you have a present to give him, haven't you?

AUNT: Here it is. I have it here.

TONY: Give it to me, and we'll put it with the others.

AUNT: Put it right on top — the others, who brought them?

TONY: The children.

ALICE: *We* did, Aunt.

AUNT: Where are they? Have they come?

TONY: Here they all are. Don't you see them?

AUNT: I see them. I'm not blind, you know. Why are you hiding them from me?

TONY: We're not hiding anything from you, Aunt — do stop it!

AUNT: You hid my hats! Did Mr Tsaldaris come?

KOSTAS: He's coming later, Aunt.

TONY: Let me show you my present. I left it to the last, because I wanted you all to be here when I opened it. The idea came from papa's manuscript that Alice read so beautifully to us.

(*Everyone follows his gestures with curiosity. He takes the cassette player off the table, presses the "play" button, and the folk song "Speak to me Birbili" is heard again. Everyone, except* IRENE *and* MANOS, *becomes roused. They make excited, cheerful noises.*)

KOSTAS: Great! Good idea, Tony — a very good idea!

MARY: A pity he can't hear it.

ALICE: How do you know he can't hear it?

GEORGE (*puts his fingers to his mouth and whistles like a brigand and, shouting* O-o-o-pa, *he pulls a handkerchief from his pocket, shakes it open and calls out*): Alice, take hold!

ALICE: Come on then!

GEORGE (*while dancing*): Take hold of it.
ALICE (*taking hold of the handkerchief*): Come one everyone — Tony . . .
TONY: Why not? (*He joins the dance.*) Irene, Mary, come and join us.
MARY (*joining the dance*): Kosta . . .
KOSTAS (*also coming in*): Irene . . .
IRENE: I don't know the Kalamata.
AUNT: Me, me, me . . .
KOSTAS: Aunt wants to join in too. Come on Aunt. Good for you.
(*With his free hand, he holds the back of Aunt's wheelchair and pulls it with him. They dance around papa's bed. The Kalamata dance with George's brigand whistling contradicts their previous upper-middle-class behaviour, and at the same time symbolises the peasant origins that they want so much to deny. They finish their dance and applaud.*)
KOSTAS: That'll have roused you, won't it papa? Did you enjoy it, Aunt?
AUNT: We used to dance a lot. My brother over there — the gentleman who is sleeping is my brother — when he began dancing he wouldn't stop. That's what they were like in the old days — always dancing — for three days, four days in a row.
ALICE: I wish I had been young then. I love dancing so much.
AUNT: People were cheerful and happy, not sullen like they are now! I was talking about this all morning to your papa.
ALICE: You were *talking* to papa?
(MANOS *comes forward.*)
AUNT: On his name day, we used to have receptions with a hundred guests. This morning, he told me about all the people he invited, and their names.
MANOS: Papa?
AUNT: My brother. A hundred gentlemen with their wives — members of parliament, sea captains, airline pilots, company directors. When he wakes up, get him to tell you about them — all in dress suits and ball gowns. You should have seen them dancing the *tsamikos*; they'd put holes in the floor.
MANOS (*dismissively*): Wonderful. How did you speak to papa?
AUNT: What do you mean? Haven't we got mouths?
TONY (*to* MANOS): Do you take her seriously?
MANOS: And do you often speak to each other?
AUNT: We pass our time — what else can we do, since they don't

ACT TWO

pay any attention to us.

TONY: That's enough. We must take papa away to his room — it's too smoky and noisy in here. (*He goes towards the back of the stage.*)

AUNT: It's his nameday. Let him see a few people.

ALICE: He'll get tired Aunt, he'll get tired.

AUNT: All morning, he's been telling me about how happy he was to be having a reception, and you're taking him out?

TONY (*to the* NURSE *who comes in*): Take him to his room.

(*The* NURSE *takes hold of the bed.*)

AUNT (*grabbing the leg of the bed*): Who do you think you are? Get your hands off him!

TONY (*sternly*): It's the nurse, Aunt. I told her to take him.

AUNT: If my brother goes, I go too. (*She holds on to the leg of the bed, and won't let them take it away.*)

TONY: Nobody says that you have to leave! But papa must go to his room. Go with him if you want, and we'll bring you back when it's time for dinner!

AUNT: I'll go, and I won't come back!

TONY: Do what you like. Nurse . . .

(*The* NURSE *takes the bed away.*)

AUNT: I never want to see any of you again. You're not children — you're freaks of nature! You don't want your father anymore, so you give him to these bitches of nurses! You've taken everything from him, and now you throw him aside. He tells *me* everything. "They're always bringing doctors to see me, and they drown me in medicine to kill me so that they can take everything. My children are murderers!"

IRENE (*hysterically, pressing her hands against her ears*): Take this mad old woman out of here!

MARY (*swoops down on the wheelchair, and grabs the back of it*): This time, she's gone too far! (*She wheels her towards the back of the stage.*)

AUNT: Where are you taking me? Where are you taking me? Help!

(*Pause.*)

TONY: Her condition is intolerable!

KOSTAS: Perhaps the change has upset her.

TONY: What change?

KOSTAS: Of surroundings.

TONY: It might interest you to know that she didn't notice the change. She still believes she is in her own house, and that you are me. She's always calling me "Kosta". She hasn't called me by *my* name once!

KOSTAS: Don't get excited. I didn't mean to upset you.

TONY: Your tone was insinuating!

KOSTAS: Rubbish!

GEORGE: She certainly sang our praises, didn't she? Ha ha.

ALICE: When people become as old as that, they lose their reason completely.

GEORGE: Or find it.

IRENE: Why are we discussing this? Why not just forget it?

TONY (*beside himself with rage*): I'll send her to a nursing home. That'll teach the senile old fool to watch her tongue!

GEORGE (*sarcastic*): Ah no — send the chronicle of our family to a nursing home?

TONY: To a nursing home, the spoilt old woman! If we hadn't wrapped her in cotton wool, she wouldn't have spewed out those preposterous fantasies. It was *you* who spoiled her like this!

KOSTAS: *You* should have improved her manners then! Was I not replaced so that you could have everything as you wanted?

TONY: It was a bit late in the day for *me* to do anything!

GEORGE: Either you let the family chronicle drivel on, or you scrap the thing and rewrite it!

TONY: Stop it, all right? You're getting on my nerves!

MARY (*coming in*): She's still giving off — shows no sign of stopping.

ALICE: Let her give off! As long as we can't hear her.

MANOS: But how did she manage to have a conversation with papa?

TONY: What are you on about now?

MANOS: She said they talk to each other every day. You all heard!

MARY: And you believed that?

MANOS: Why would I not believe it? Have I any evidence to the contrary?

TONY: Evidence? You're mad! If you believe Aunt's ravings, go and keep her company.

MANOS: Perhaps I'll do just that — I might learn something.

TONY: Suit yourself. She's in her room. Go — take her. I give her to you — she's all yours!

MARY: Don't get worked up! You know what Manos is like.

MANOS: No, he doesn't know me. Nobody knows me.

TONY: That's true. You're a very shady character to say the least!

ACT TWO

MANOS: Don't ever say such a stupid thing to me again.
TONY: I'll say worse than that, Mr Bloody High and Mighty.
GEORGE: Easy.
TONY: Didn't you hear the scheming rogue? He suspects that papa can talk, and we're hiding it from him. (*To* KOSTAS): You try convincing him that papa has *not* spoken for years.
KOSTAS: Leave me out of this.
TONY: You know better than anyone else that papa is in a permanent state of dementia.
KOSTAS: Don't pressure me. I won't tell lies!
TONY: Are you talking drivel now too?
KOSTAS: Not in the least. During the time I was looking after papa, I couldn't say for certain that he conversed regularly, but he did say something. He wasn't completely silent.
TONY: That's impossible.
KOSTAS: You asked, and I answered.
ALICE: I'm a witness. I heard him speak. He opened his eyes and recognised me. He even smiled at me.
KOSTAS: Let me explain. I must emphasise that he didn't say much, nor was he always coherent. But quite often, he had lucid moments when one could exchange a few words with him.
MARY: This is news to me!
TONY: And to me!
MARY: Is it? How could he suddenly achieve mental clarity? By himself?
KOSTAS: Of course. I never saw the Holy Ghost fluttering above him.
TONY: And why weren't we told this?
KOSTAS: What? That papa can speak? Since I never told you he can't, why should I tell you out of the blue that he can?
MANOS: So, Aunt is right.
ALICE: Certainly. Well, up to a point — eh Kosta?
KOSTAS: I don't understand, unless something has changed since he's been *here*. Perhaps this change hasn't done him any good.
MARY: He has never been as well as he is now! His colour has never been this good before!
KOSTAS: He *has* colour. I noticed that.
TONY: Listen. I don't like people suspecting me. I detest that more than anything in the world. I can see that there's a conspiracy here. Whoever has something to say against me — say it! (*To* MANOS): You — say it!

MANOS: Don't tempt me.

TONY: You don't need any encouragement!

MANOS: Some other time.

TONY: Say it! You suspect that I'm conversing with papa, don't you? That I'm plotting to revise the will at your expense? Exactly as you suspected Kostas before me, and just as you would suspect anyone else! And all this, *not* because you have a trace of moral integrity, but because you were born with hang-ups — you were born paranoid.

MANOS: Say what you like. It's all talk. I have plenty of evidence.

(*It's as if a thunderbolt had struck.*)

TONY (*astounded*): Who did you get it from? Your police spies? Go on, you miserable bastard — I'm not afraid of you. If you have evidence, let's see it!

MARY: What are the rest of you doing? Why don't you say something? How can you let him slander Tony like this?

ALICE: Kostas got the same treatment.

KOSTAS: Don't involve me. I don't need an advocate.

IRENE: May *I* suggest something?

TONY: Suggest what you like! I'm finished with this discussion. It's absurd, petty and above all disrespectful. We are here for papa's nameday!

GEORGE: Stop it! Stop it! How much lower can this get? Do you realise what we've said to each other? And now you're backing off like two whores fighting in an alley! (*To* MANOS): Have you evidence against him or not?

MANOS: I don't make idle statements.

GEORGE: Ah, you haven't any evidence. You need a bloody good beating! (*To* TONY): Are you just going to stand there and take this?

TONY: What he says doesn't interest me.

GEORGE: If you have any self-respect it *should* interest you!

TONY: I'm listening.

MANOS: All this time, he's been making his stockbroker buy the firm's shares. He buys up any that are available, and conveniently ends up with them at any opportune moment. Do you deny it?

TONY: I can justify that.

MANOS (*to* KOSTAS): Is there a rule that we must all have the same number of shares?

KOSTAS: A decision was made by the Board of Governors on the

ACT TWO

9th of March 1969.

MANOS: Is this some kind of scam?

TONY: I said I would justify it.

GEORGE: You had another piece of evidence. You said so.

MANOS: You should have seen the staff changes he made from the day he became director! He has put *his* people in all the top jobs. He does whatever he likes without anyone being able to question it.

TONY: So what? Every director does that. He chooses people he can depend on.

MANOS: You're lying! Tomorrow morning, I can give you all proof of the forgeries he has committed! He has changed the dates on invoices which were issued in your day (*turning to* KOSTAS) to make it appear that sales have increased from the time he took over. And what's more, he has kept papa here for months pretending he doesn't talk to him. And all the time, he's making him do whatever he wants! We thought he was the best — he's nothing but a gangster, as they say in America!

(TONY *grabs a chair and leaps forward to hit him, but* GEORGE *and* KOSTAS *restrain him while the women shriek.*)

TONY: Leave me alone! Let go of me!

KOSTAS: Not so we can butcher one another.

GEORGE: Give me the chair. Give me the chair.

ALICE: I wish I'd never been born to see this! Throw the swindler out!

MARY (*pointing at* MANOS): He's going to bankrupt us. He'll ruin us all!

IRENE: May they cut off my legs if I ever set foot in Greece again. Give me my share and I'll leave this Godforsaken country!

(*The men have taken the chair from* TONY, *and have set him down on an armchair.*)

KOSTAS: It should never have come to this.

TONY: Listen to that! Gangster . . .

KOSTAS: Calm down.

TONY: This fascist calls *me* a gangster!

GEORGE: Never mind him. We will judge what kind of person you are! Now, we know about the staff you shuffled around. We weren't waiting for *him* to tell us! But as regards the date changes on the invoices — well that's fraud. If he wanted, he could have you locked up.

IRENE: Prison? That would disgrace the lot of us!

MARY (*to* GEORGE): Don't exaggerate. Who appointed you as magistrate? Did you see the fraud with your own eyes? Did *you* see the papers? Do we have to call our brother a crook just because that wimp says so?

GEORGE: You're right — he is a wimp.

MARY (*to* KOSTAS): You're the eldest. Say something!

KOSTAS: Let the accused speak. Why doesn't he speak? I'm totally confident that he can defend himself better than anyone else.

TONY (*rising*): Don't interrupt me again. I've been subjected to a barrage of insults in my own house. I think you can do me the honour of not interrupting. Yes, I *did* change the dates on the invoices! Yes, I *do* buy shares beyond the limit we agreed on! But my intention was not the swindle that this fascist suspects — and I'll explain to you later what I mean when I call him a fascist! What he calls a swindle, I call self-sacrifice. From the day I assumed the directorship — and don't forget that you all chose me — you began to suspect and distrust me. Things that were said about Kostas during his time as director have also been said about me. I realised immediately, because I *wasn't* born yesterday, that whoever becomes director will have his grave dug by the rest.

KOSTAS: How perceptive of you.

TONY: I asked you not to interrupt me. Well then, it's very obvious that this post can't be filled by a saint! And since I'm not a saint, as none of us is, I had to watch my back any way I could. Not to save myself, but the integrity and security of the firm. It's inevitable that whoever is director feels that he and the firm are one!

GEORGE: Would you like a drink of water?

TONY: This is no time for jokes! I've no intention of becoming a dictator, because I'm a born democrat. I am determined to do everything I can in the name of democracy. But to be able to do all this, you must pour cold water on your conscience, sacrifice your feelings and risk being labelled power-mad. Otherwise you will never be strong enough to lay down the law and put any idiot in his place who . . .

ALICE: What kind of attitude is this?

TONY (*to* KOSTAS): See the difference between you and me? I don't neglect my duties out of cowardice. Yes, I *did* change the dates on the invoices, so that, as the new director, I could negotiate a better deal with the bank. How's this likely to harm you? I did

ACT TWO

increase my shares in order to strengthen my position, because I know you can dismiss me just as easily as you elected me. You would let us fall into anarchy, instability and liquidation! Isn't it wise to take risks when competition is lying in wait to tear us apart? How can I govern with Christian charity, when our dominance in the marketplace depends on my dominance in the firm?

MANOS: And he calls *me* a fascist!

TONY: Shut up! Experience teaches . . . you've made me lose my train of thought . . .

GEORGE: Concentrate.

TONY: . . . teaches . . . that the strength of the firm has, until now, been preserved by illicit means. The first offender was our beloved and venerable papa! Do you want to throw everything our history has taught us onto the trash heap? Throw it away then. *I* won't. I'll always be papa's *real* son! If my course in becoming a forger and increasing my shares on the side upsets you all, then we can say goodbye to our authority in the marketplace! Please try to realise that I made the sacrifice of soiling my hands for the common good. You may be disgusted by all this — I can see that you are — but the situation called for it. The reality is that *you* set the wheels in motion. And if you can't accept that without throwing up, then we'll all be under the thumb of this bloody fascist. (*Pointing to* MANOS): He undermined Kostas in order to take the first step — now, he's undermining me to take the second. The same will happen to a third, and then his final solution will be to wipe us all out. You have escaped from *us*, but you'll never escape from *him*. Decide for yourselves.

MARY: There's nothing to decide. Things will stay as they are. (*To* MANOS): *Tony*'s not going to decide for everybody.

KOSTAS: How can you speak for all of us? Listen Tony, despite the fact that *I* was accused in the same way . . .

ALICE: We have to pay for everything that happens in this life. Religion . . .

KOSTAS (*irritated*): Don't shit on what I'm saying!

ALICE: How could you speak to me like that?

KOSTAS: First one of you women, then the other. You all butt in like farts. You force me to use words that I'm not in the habit of using.

IRENE: So now we're all farts.

KOSTAS (*to* ALICE): Say your piece. Say it.

ALICE: Religion has taught us something very true. One day, each of us will climb to our Golgotha — we all have our Judas.

KOSTAS (*sternly*): Tony, you were vile to me on the day I was accused, but I won't stoop to your level. I'll take no interest in the evidence Manos has against you, and to which you have given no real answer! (*Mildly*): Incurable sentimentalist that I am, I will confine myself to papa's condition. Who put make-up on him?

ALICE: What?

IRENE: Make-up?

KOSTAS: Somebody put make-up on him to improve his colour! I demand to know who committed this forgery. The other one was a shambles compared to *this* masterpiece.

MARY: I did it!

ALICE: I thought I smelt something odd when I kissed him.

IRENE: It's bad luck — in America they put make-up on the dead.

GEORGE: Oh come on. My God, what'll we hear next in this house?

KOSTAS (*to* TONY): Were you involved in this? I mean did you put the make-up on together?

TONY: We didn't mean any harm.

MARY: He looked a bit pale — we said we'd do it so's you wouldn't be worried.

KOSTAS: There's no excuse for it under any circumstances. This... this masquerade finally shows what kind of animal you really are, Tony! I say that papa should be transferred to somebody else's house as quickly as possible! I don't know what the others think.

GEORGE: I'm the first to agree! We're not turning papa into a clown.

ALICE: I agree too, the poor soul.

MANOS: That's fine, as far as I'm concerned.

ALICE: Irene?

IRENE: Let somebody else take him. (*To* ALICE): Would *you* not?

ALICE: Gladly, but I have only a small house and no servants.

IRENE: Well, I'm abroad most of the time.

KOSTAS: I think George ought to look after him.

GEORGE (*terrified*): Are you looking for a *new* victim?

KOSTAS: He *is* your father. It is your duty.

GEORGE: You're right, he is my father, but what happens with the rest of you after I take him?

ACT TWO

ALICE: You are *so* good.

GEORGE: And Kostas was good, and Tony was good!

KOSTAS: You can be sure that we have total confidence in you.

IRENE: He must take over the directorship.

TONY: We'll see about that! It's not that simple!

KOSTAS: Considering the evidence we have against you, it would be wise to keep your mouth shut! George *should* direct the firm for the time being.

GEORGE: Are you asking if I agree to this?

KOSTAS: It's your duty! Otherwise we might as well go home and let the whole thing go to hell!

ALICE: Do it for papa!

KOSTAS: The staff all like and respect you. We'll stand by you. With all this instability, we need a man of your character to maintain the balance. Can't you see that?

GEORGE: Let me think about it first. But I warn you, I have no ambition to be director, nor do I want to be wealthier! I prefer to be free from worry, and live my life like a human being. I like an easy life. You know me. If I go into this venture, it'll be to close the sewer we've opened here. But God help us if I have to face any more conspiracies — I'll go mad! If anyone so much as touches me, I'll strike back. After all, I *am* a peasant. I'm not the aristocracy, you know?

TONY: I can't agree to this, and I'll tell you why, even though we're more used to hearing accusations from *this* gentleman. (*Pointing to* MANOS): He is, as we know, his own judge and jury. (*To* GEORGE): Your son is a Maoist!

GEORGE: A Maoist?

MARY: Nonsense . . .

TONY (*to* GEORGE): I know *you're* all right, but your son and heir?

GEORGE: Leave my son out of this! What *he* does shouldn't reflect on me.

TONY: I cannot accept a director with a Maoist son. We put our clerks and workers through a fine sieve. We have dismissed people because the police informed us that they had relatives in the prison camps. And now we're going to have a leader who has kept his son's Maoist beliefs a secret. Are you all out of your minds?

KOSTAS: Is he really a Maoist?

TONY (*pointing to* MANOS): In the company's files, he has a photograph of a communist meeting, in which George's son can be seen holding Mao's red book.

KOSTAS (*to* MANOS): Have you such a photograph?

MANOS: I have.

MARY: Well then, you may as well know that I saw him putting up posters as red as tomatoes.

GEORGE: My son?

MARY: In Patisia Street.

KOSTAS: George, this is very serious! I'm sorry, but with a leftist son, your credentials are no longer clean.

GEORGE: I had no idea. I swear to you by all that I hold sacred. He kept it hidden from me, the little bastard. But let's say that it's . . . Do *I* have to pay for my son's beliefs?

TONY: He's your only son. How can he not influence you?

MARY: It's impossible.

GEORGE: That's enough. All right, my son *is* a Maoist. And your son, what has he been doing in Germany for so many years?

MARY: You know very well that he's studying.

GEORGE: Still?

MARY: He's doing postgraduate work.

GEORGE: Nonsense! He's writing articles for that journal — what do they call it . . .

MANOS: "Socialist Viewpoints".

MARY: He may be a socialist, but he doesn't write for a journal.

GEORGE: This journal is printed in Athens. Would you like to see it?

MANOS: I have as many copies as you want.

MARY: In any case, he is *not* a leftist.

KOSTAS: He *is*, Madam.

ALICE: *I* didn't know this.

KOSTAS: These communists and socialists are all the same, and they all have one purpose in mind — to overthrow our economic and social system! So don't just talk about *his* son. Go and straighten out your own son first.

MARY: So, have you straightened out *your* son?

KOSTAS: Not one more word about *him*!

TONY: No, not one word.

KOSTAS: I mean it.

TONY: You cannot apply one standard to others and another to yourself!

KOSTAS: Watch what you're saying, or I'll tell them about your daughter.

TONY: My daughter did *not* take part in the revolt at the Polytechnic!

ALICE: However, your daughter was a hippie, and still is.

TONY: My daughter is a woman. She'll get married one day and change her ways.

ALICE: If she had wanted to, she'd have changed by now. It's been years since she left home to live by herself.

TONY: Kostas is threatening to blow the whistle on my daughter for being independent. That's hardly political anarchy.

ALICE: I don't know what it is. I do know that she was protesting to me about not wanting a penny from you — because according to her, your money is dirty. She's working for a publisher, and will make enough to go and live in a pacifist commune in Holland! She told me that as soon as she inherits, she'll give everything away — I don't remember where.

TONY: Call her depraved. Call her a tramp, but that isn't a social danger like . . .

KOSTAS: It is the worst danger of all. Such ingratitude and insults from our own flesh and blood. It's unheard of! These hippie parasites are all sponging off us. A leftist may become right wing one day, but an anarchist *never* settles down!

TONY: You mean *your* son has settled down?

KOSTAS: My son was never a leftist.

MARY: Was he at the Polytechnic or wasn't he?

KOSTAS: He was outside, like thousands of others.

ALICE: And I went to see it. Does that make me a leftist?

TONY: Your son was inside making bombs.

KOSTAS: That's all rumour.

TONY: Was he inside or wasn't he? Tell the truth!

ALICE: But everyone accepted the protest. The government even sent a wreath.

MANOS: The government did *not* accept it. To their shame, they had to swallow their pride and use delay tactics. It's true what Tony says. His son *was* inside, and playing a leading role.

TONY: He was in the very middle of it all, with the ammunition!

MARY: When he was arrested, I went with him to the army headquarters to see the Commandant. Because I knew him, he intervened to have your son released immediately.

KOSTAS: He was carried away by it all — but my son is not and never was a leftist! And after the Polytechnic, he never got drawn into anything.

TONY: You're not very well informed.
KOSTAS: As a leftist?
TONY: No, about your son!
KOSTAS: You've wounded me.
TONY: I've also been wounded.
GEORGE: We all have.
   (*Pause.*)
KOSTAS: Me first then — besides I'm the oldest and ought to set an example — could whoever knows anything at all about my son's activities please tell me about them. (*He takes out a notebook and pencil.*) No illusions. It's time to find out where we stand. Tell me what you know about my rascal of a son. Don't leave anything out.
TONY (*to* MANOS): Could we forget our differences and talk like civilised human beings?
MANOS: What do you want to know?
TONY: Tell him.
MANOS (*to* KOSTAS): How about tomorrow morning at eleven?
KOSTAS: Why not now?
MANOS: I must have my notes.
KOSTAS: I'll be in your office at eleven o'clock sharp.
MANOS: I'll be expecting you.
KOSTAS: Thank you.
GEORGE (*with notebook and pencil in his hands, he also asks* MARY): Where did you say he was putting up posters?
MARY: In Patisia Street, at the Business College.
GEORGE (*taking a note*): When was this?
MARY: Before Easter, I think — about that time.
GEORGE (*taking a note*): Alone, or with others?
MARY: There were two, maybe three. I can't remember very well.
GEORGE (*to* MANOS): May I have that photograph?
MANOS: Of course.
GEORGE: Thank you.
MARY: And I want that journal from you.
GEORGE: You'll get it.
TONY (*with an almost angry cry*): The bitch — the slut!
ALICE: Tony dear . . .
TONY: I have no other child. How can she do this to me? What'll I do now? What hopes have I?
   (MARY *bursts into tears.*)
IRENE (*sarcastic*): You're crying! Are you really crying?

ACT TWO

KOSTAS (*flaring up*): It's heart-breaking. We toil, we build, we struggle. We are in a constant battle with the rest of society. We've even sacrificed family love and unity. We do everything to ensure that papa's work is handed down intact! And where do we end up? Saying that it's all been in vain? In the end, we have no children! No children and no future! So, since we are the last of our kind, why tear one another apart? I suppose it's something that we've understood this, even if it *is* late in the day. At least let's know who will be the first to overthrow us.

MANOS: Well, from now on . . .

IRENE: What are you all saying? I don't understand a word.

MARY: Go back to sleep.

TONY: I feel the need to ask your forgiveness — not that I feel guilty. I simply feel the need.

ALICE: I'm confused.

MANOS: That's enough talk. What exactly are we deciding here?

KOSTAS (*to* TONY): Do me a favour. Go and bring papa in — and bring a newspaper — any newspaper. It's not important.

TONY: Why do you want him?

KOSTAS: From now on, I can't have secrets from any of you. Bring him in.

(TONY *goes to bring papa in.*)

MANOS: Why do you want to bring papa? What can *he* do?

ALICE: Don't tell me that we haven't been enlightened by papa's spirit! He sensed that we weren't getting on well, and has inspired this reconciliation. Have you got his glasses?

KOSTAS: Whose?

ALICE: Papa's. Have you got them with you?

KOSTAS: No, but we don't need glasses. On second thoughts, I'll put mine on him. He won't know the difference.

IRENE: But what are you going to do?

KOSTAS: Come — everyone sit over here so that you can all see.

(TONY *brings papa in.*)

KOSTAS: We have to raise him up a bit.

(*They raise him up.*)

TONY: Here's the paper.

KOSTAS: Good, now sit down.

(*The scene rather resembles a conjuring act.*)

KOSTAS: Now pay attention. I will prove to you that we are not alone, that we are not without a leader. Papa, the source of our strength, has not abandoned us. Pay attention. (*He puts his own glasses on papa, and begins to draw the paper down over his nose, as in the earlier scene*): Papa, your paper. Papa, can you hear me? Your paper, your favourite paper. Smell it, papa. Take a breath. Come on . . . good. Go on, papa. That's good — and another breath. Smell it again. Take a deep breath. Keep going. Don't stop. Now open it. Open your fingers. Hold it tight — with both hands. Come on, good. Good, papa.

(*The old man grasps the paper with both hands.*)

KOSTAS: Now your eyes — your eyes papa. Open one — that's right! And the other, papa — and the other.

ALL: Go on, papa!

KOSTAS: He's opened his eyes.

ALL: Well done, papa!

(*They all applaud.*)

KOSTAS (*moved*): What did I tell you? Everything's going to be all right. We may no longer have children, but we still have papa!

LIGHTS OUT

—— THE END ——

IBSENLAND

FOREWORD

At the time when I was discovering the theatre, Ibsen was the writer who could totally absorb me when I first read and then re-read his plays. Even after I had read and been enraptured by other neo-classicists, I felt that for me, Ibsen's characters, more than any others, could talk, breathe, think, react to one another. In Ibsen, I saw for the first time, a world of stage characters who are so real that they rend the heart, as do Chekhov's creatures; who assert their independence so naturally, rebelling against the confinement of their theatrical existence, as do Pirandello's characters.

My first theatre school, the one that taught me the basics, as we say, basics which I believe in to this day, was "Ibsenland". This, at the time, was what I liked to call the theatre of Ibsen.

This one-act play, *Ibsenland*, is a free study based on *Ghosts*, and on two of the chief characters in that play, Pastor Manders and Mrs Alving. Its story is a companion piece to Ibsen's story.

If I were a theoretician of the theatre, my persistent inclination to examine these characters and their tragic course, would have been conveyed in a commentary. However, I'm not a theoretician, so I kept company with them, trying to imagine their prehistory – situations and events in their past which they mention as being significant landmarks in their lives — and I have presented these in the form from which they originate, the theatrical form. As is natural, since I have attempted to guess their behaviour at other times and other moments in their lives, differences between my characters and their prototypes are inevitable. Besides, my intention was neither to produce a condensed version of the play, nor indeed to add to an already replete and great work; *Ibsenland* is simply a creative study, an exercise, a game of fantasy where arbitrariness informs all that is said and done.

I<small>AKOVOS</small> K<small>AMBANELLIS</small>

IBSENLAND

THE CHARACTERS IN THE PLAY

NIGHTWATCHMAN:	formerly a prompter, before that an actor
VOICE:	of another nightwatchman.
MANDERS:	the pastor from Ibsen's *Ghosts* and also the actor who plays him
OLAF:	Pastor Manders in his youth
HELENA:	the youthful Mrs Alving
MRS ALVING:	Helena at the age of forty-five
OSVALD:	Mrs Alving's son as he is in *Ghosts*

The stage is in darkness.

A light shines from a NIGHTWATCHMAN'S *torch at the left entrance to the stage. He crosses to the right, and disappears into the wings. He turns on the bright electric rehearsal light. On the now lit-up stage, we see the remains of a set for* Ghosts, *which is in the process of being dismantled; some of the furniture is still in place.* Pastor MANDERS *sits on a couch. The* NIGHTWATCHMAN *appears, carrying an improvised table, on which he has placed an old briefcase. He leaves the briefcase against the flat, stage right, at the proscenium arch, and goes into the wings again. He comes back, carrying a chair and a table lamp. He sits down on the chair, plugs the lamp into a socket which is in behind the proscenium. He switches it on, and places it on the table. He goes into the wings again, turns out the rehearsal light, comes back, and sits behind the table. He has a view of the stage in front of him. From the briefcase, he takes out a book, a bottle of beer, a plastic cup, and a large sandwich wrapped in tinfoil.*

The ease with which he moves about the stage shows familiarity with it, and, because of his work, familiarity with the dark in general.

As he begins to take the things out of the briefcase, someone speaks to him from the stalls. He replies with restrained annoyance.

VOICE: Hungry?
NIGHTWATCHMAN: It's gone two o'clock.
VOICE: I've just eaten, myself. Nicely settled up there, eh?
NIGHTWATCHMAN: An old habit.
VOICE: Were there many in tonight?
NIGHTWATCHMAN: Packed.
VOICE: Ah, of course, the last performance.
NIGHTWATCHMAN: Nonsense! They like the play!
VOICE: Have they started to take down the set already?
NIGHTWATCHMAN: Can't you see?
VOICE: And when . . . ?
NIGHTWATCHMAN: There'll be another set from Tuesday.
VOICE: Good play?
NIGHTWATCHMAN: Good, but it won't be like this one.
VOICE: Really, eh?
NIGHTWATCHMAN: Have you checked all the doors?
VOICE: All of them.
NIGHTWATCHMAN: Have another look.
VOICE: Again?
NIGHTWATCHMAN: Will you listen to me? I've been thirty one years in this place. Anything that happens — the nightwatchmen are to blame. (*He opens the book, and the bottle of beer, and begins to eat.*)
MANDERS: Was he an actor too at one time?
NIGHTWATCHMAN: *You're here!* Pardon me, I didn't see you. (*Arranging his provisions*): Was he an actor? Not at all! He's never acted in his life!
MANDERS: Why did *you* give it up?
NIGHTWATCHMAN: *I* didn't give it up. I knew very well that I wouldn't be given more than half a dozen words as an actor, so I became a prompter instead. I did thirteen years as a prompter, but it affected me — psychologically. And it wasn't a permanent job; they could sack me at any time. When I saw they were taking on permanent nightwatchmen, I made up my mind. Nightwatchman it was — either that, or find myself totally outside the theatre. I couldn't have stood the separation. It would have broken my heart.
MANDERS: I understand.

NIGHTWATCHMAN: In a play — I don't remember now which one — someone refers to "all the mad failures". He could be right. I don't know, but mad or deluded, they're driven by their passions! Whereas the successful become lethargic.
MANDERS: Not all.
NIGHTWATCHMAN: You're right, not all. There are exceptions — few though!
MANDERS: Very few.
NIGHTWATCHMAN: The theatre isn't a nine to five job! It demands all your time and energy — twenty four hours a day.
MANDERS: It's hardly a job!
NIGHTWATCHMAN: I'm very sorry this play's over.
MANDERS: Yes, because it isn't just a play!
NIGHTWATCHMAN: And what a role you had, pastor!
MANDERS: Don't I know that.
NIGHTWATCHMAN: How do you think it went this evening?
MANDERS: Were you not here?
NIGHTWATCHMAN: Do you think I'd miss the last performance!
MANDERS: Fair enough . . . probably not. Well, there was absolutely no difference! It was the same as yesterday, and the day before yesterday, and as always. They heartily applauded my dear colleague who plays Mrs Alving, as well as that young puppy who plays Osvald, and even our good friend who plays that rascal Engstrand.
NIGHTWATCHMAN: It was the same for you. I tell you, I was here. I heard them.
MANDERS: Just a minute. We're coming to me! They also heartily applauded that conceited little madam who plays Regina, and yes, me as well. There is, however, an essential difference: they feel obliged to applaud me, only because I'm perfect in my role. And now that I come to mention it, when have they ever seen a better Manders? Yet, it's very obvious that deep down, they dislike me!
NIGHTWATCHMAN: No, it isn't really like that.
MANDERS: Do you know better than I do? I see it after every performance! The others' dressing-rooms are full of people from the audience, all open-mouthed, wanting to meet them, to kiss them — asking for autographs and photographs! The few who come to me are only being polite!
NIGHTWATCHMAN: I'm not so sure about that.
MANDERS: And not one of them asks for anything! Not one of

them has the slightest doubt about me! Even in my own dressing-room, they see me simply as a repellent character, and that's that!

NIGHTWATCHMAN: That is simply not true.

MANDERS: They're stupid and unjust!

NIGHTWATCHMAN: Then again, in my thirty one years in the theatre, I've heard them all say that the audience is the final judge!

MANDERS (*flaring up*): What is it a judge of? What exactly is it judging? It knows only how to be biased. It listens and pays attention only to the actors it likes — the so-called sympathetic characters in the play! But does it see me? Me, Manders, does it pay attention to me? Has it ever thought of me as a person? Has it ever wondered what *I* went through, what all this business cost *me*? Never! It sees me only as a narrow-minded and dangerous pastor! Is *this* the final judgement?

NIGHTWATCHMAN: It's so one dimensional.

MANDERS: Instead of stopping to think what really happened, it blithely throws the responsibility onto me. It must have a culprit, so it chooses Manders.

NIGHTWATCHMAN: Don't upset yourself.

MANDERS: The idiots! Of course, if you can blame one person for what happened, it's easy. But if two or three are guilty, the audience has to exert its brain a little to understand exactly who is to blame! And maybe the audience would feel uneasy too! So, call Manders the culprit right from the word go, and have done with it! May I have one of your cigarettes? In other words, I'm the only one . . .

NIGHTWATCHMAN (*handing him the packet of cigarettes*): You don't have to ask.

MANDERS: . . . who harmed others? Nobody harmed me? (*Taking the cigarette*): But if, my dear friend, there's one culprit for every evil in the world, then why should we get upset? It's simple. We can even reform him!

NIGHTWATCHMAN (*offering him his lighter*): Need a light?

MANDERS: Aren't these simplifications ridiculous? And at my expense!

NIGHTWATCHMAN: Do you need a light? Pastor, *I* haven't any spec . . .

MANDERS: Thanks.

NIGHTWATCHMAN: . . . special education, except for my experience in the theatre and my passion for it. I see all the plays without exception, and any I like, I see several times! For example, I already know "Ghosts", yet I saw almost all the performances this time! Now that we're on the subject . . . (*He hesitates.*)

MANDERS: Speak your mind.

NIGHTWATCHMAN: May I ask you a personal question?

MANDERS: Go on.

NIGHTWATCHMAN: What happened previously between you and Mrs Alving?

MANDERS (*a silence*): A very pertinent question! Yes — but you're obviously not stupid! You can't guess what could have happened?

NIGHTWATCHMAN: I *can*, pastor, I can well imagine.

MANDERS: Unfortunately, it's a very delicate subject. I can't compromise a lady! Even though it's precisely this delicacy and silence on my part that puts me in the dock!

NIGHTWATCHMAN: But she told you straight out . . .

MANDERS: She is a woman. I am a minister of the church. The contest is unequal.

NIGHTWATCHMAN: Yes, but you're also a man.

MANDERS: I told you, it's a delicate subject. Don't press me!

NIGHTWATCHMAN: All right then, pastor. Either speak or don't complain.

MANDERS (*troubled*): I haven't talked about it since! No matter what a torment it is to be the only one who knows something!

NIGHTWATCHMAN: All the more reason to talk about it.

MANDERS (*after another pause*): Can I at least be sure that nothing of what you hear will go any further?

NIGHTWATCHMAN: If you have the slightest doubt . . .

MANDERS: Do you know why I'm so hesitant? As you'll see when I begin to tell you, whatever I do turns against me in the end!

NIGHTWATCHMAN: I give you my word of honour! What more can I do?

MANDERS: Listen then. Helena Sorensen, later Mrs Sigurd Alving, was an adorable creature — beautiful, sensitive, ethereal.

NIGHTWATCHMAN: Ah, I can believe it — since even now . . . !

MANDERS: Imagine her at eighteen, nineteen years old.

NIGHTWATCHMAN: She must have been exquisite! Did you know each other when you were so young?

MANDERS: Since we were children. We played together, Sigurd Alving, she, and I. When we were growing up, we separated for some years because of our studies. Helena went to Christiania, to a girls' school, Sigurd to the Military Academy, and myself to Theological College. When we came back to Rosenvold, quite grown up already, and Helena of marrying age, we didn't see each other as much as before — and never alone. Except when we met by chance — or, as if by chance.

NIGHTWATCHMAN: "Or, as if by chance!" That's intriguing, pastor.

MANDERS: Naturally, as a cleric just starting out, and, I have to confess, proud of the cloth, I had to be very careful about my former friendships with girls, and especially with Helena.

(HELENA *comes on stage with a parasol and a bunch of flowering esparto grass. She stands still, contriving the "chance encounter" with the young* OLAF Manders, *who appears a little later.*)

MANDERS: I'm going to confess something that not even she ever knew about. I wrote poems to her. I even set two or three to music.

NIGHTWATCHMAN: You're musical?

MANDERS: I play the church organ very well. I would catch myself singing hymns to the Virgin, and thinking about Helena.

NIGHTWATCHMAN (*with emotion and wonder*): Really? I would never have imagined it!

MANDERS: If I'd wanted, I could have asked her to marry me, and become Mrs Pastor Manders, instead of the wife of Chamberlain and aide-de-camp Alving.

NIGHTWATCHMAN: You could have, pastor. And you didn't?

MANDERS: I had made the decision not to marry.

NIGHTWATCHMAN: You made that decision on your own?

MANDERS: Yes, on my own.

NIGHTWATCHMAN: For what reason? A young, handsome man like you didn't have to play second fiddle to anyone, in my opinion.

MANDERS: I'll explain later . . . or? Yes, better to wait.

(OLAF *enters. The "chance encounter" takes place.* HELENA *sits down on the stage carpet — which is supposed to be grass in a thicket. She takes the young man's hand, and persuades him to sit down as well. At the same time, the* OLDER MANDERS *continues his narrative.*)

MANDERS: Anyway, this so-called chance encounter that you see was not at all by chance. She was supposedly passing by the grounds where the church and rectory are. She saw me coming out, and stopped to tell me the news.

HELENA: I've had a proposal of marriage.

OLAF (*taking the esparto, and examining it closely*): Look, it has flowered already!

HELENA: Olaf, did you hear what I said? I have received a proposal of marriage.

OLAF: That's only natural, isn't it? You're a sought-after bride — isn't that what they say?

HELENA: Stop teasing, Olaf.

OLAF: I'm not teasing. That's what they all say about you.

HELENA: I want to be myself and nothing else.

OLAF: And what is your real self, Helena? Do you know?

HELENA: Of course I know.

OLAF: It's very important that you know. You have many opportunities to do whatever *you* want with your life.

HELENA: Really, Olaf?

OLAF: Yes, Helena, so I believe.

HELENA: Aren't you going to ask who proposed to me?

OLAF: I think I know — Sigurd Alving.

HELENA (*surprised*): Yes! Who told you?

OLAF (*with false animation*): Congratulations then!

HELENA: Don't be in such a hurry. I haven't decided anything yet.

OLAF: Really? Then don't delay. Someone else'll take him from you.

HELENA: Olaf, you like to joke, and why shouldn't you, but not now, please.

OLAF: All right then.

HELENA: Tell me how you knew. Did you see Sigurd? Did he tell you?

OLAF: Nobody told me. I knew it, Helena. I've known it since I was a child.

HELENA: What do you mean by that?

OLAF: I always had the idea that one day you would marry Sigurd — that you would become Mrs Alving.

HELENA: So you're a prophet too!

OLAF: I didn't need to be. He was taller, stronger, more handsome, and enormously rich. When he was ten he had his own horse. Besides, I used to hear the grownups say that one day, you and Sigurd would marry.

HELENA: Well well! So, they had all decided among themselves — even at that time?

OLAF: Such dreams have their own rules, and they aren't so

unreasonable, you know! "The Alving family, the Sorensen family." One name goes with the other. Our social scales are balanced.

HELENA: I couldn't care less!

(*A short silence.*)

OLAF (*nervously peering at the esparto grass*): So it's flowered already. It's been a long time since I went there.

HELENA: Be honest with me, Olaf. Do you think the same way?

OLAF: Why would I think otherwise? Really, I don't understand why you're not happy about it. I thought you liked Sigurd.

HELENA: I only liked to dance with him. Sigurd dances very well! But if you think I really ought to like him, then I promise you, I'll think about it!

OLAF: Yes, Helena, you ought to think about it. I don't believe there's anyone better for you.

HELENA: I thought there was.

OLAF: There isn't. Sigurd himself proposed to you. (*Again with false animation*): Tell me, what exactly did he say to you? I'm curious.

MANDERS (*to the* NIGHTWATCHMAN): No, Sigurd didn't say anything to her. His parents spoke to her mother and she spoke to Helena. From that moment, she felt almost panic-stricken. She couldn't bear to stay in the house. She would go out and walk for hours alone on the mountainside.

NIGHTWATCHMAN (*with anxious eagerness*): Pastor, may I interrupt you? For Heaven's sake, it's clear as daylight that he's making a mistake. There's something very serious that he doesn't understand. (*He is turning towards* OLAF.)

MANDERS (*rather sternly*): Come back here. We were talking!

NIGHTWATCHMAN: But she hasn't come just to tell you her news. There's something else that she wants you to understand.

MANDERS: Do you take me for a fool? Or do you think I'm deaf? Didn't you see what an effort I made to pretend I didn't understand! While all the time, I was taking in every word she was saying — and I was suffering, because I saw that the moment had come when someone else would marry her.

NIGHTWATCHMAN: Because you should have married her!

MANDERS: But I told you. I had decided not to marry!

NIGHTWATCHMAN: Then why did you let her have false hopes? Why didn't you tell her?

MANDERS: Don't ask me. I can't remember. I don't . . . Perhaps I didn't want her to know!

NIGHTWATCHMAN: That was wrong! I fear that what I've heard up to now, has been a bad start, pastor! And then . . . ?

HELENA: Yes, Olaf, this Sunday evening.

OLAF: So your mother and your aunts have decided on it before you have?

HELENA: No, they would never do that. Nor are the Alvings inviting us so that we can give them a reply. From what I've heard they've even invited other people. It's not unlikely that they'll invite you too.

OLAF: Not at all unlikely. They'll want me to play the piano.

HELENA: Don't be sarcastic. You and Sigurd were inseparable friends.

OLAF: But that's why I'm so delighted for you — and you mistake it for joking. It's like a fairy tale. "My childhood friend Sigurd, the servant of God, marries my childhood friend Helena, the handmaiden of God" — and I really mean it when I say I'd like to be the first to congratulate you, to wish you . . .

HELENA: And this is your advice too, is it Olaf?

OLAF: In any case, you'll get married *some* day.

HELENA: I used to dream of being with someone I would want with all my heart.

OLAF: "With all your heart" — what does that mean? What you're saying is unrealistic!

HELENA Since one marries only once.

OLAF: All the more reason why one should look at it logically, coolly. If you told me that you had fallen passionately in love, I would do everything I could to bring you to your senses. We know only too well how these tempests of the heart, these deluded passions, end! Do you and Sigurd see each other often?

HELENA: Not often, mostly in Christiania. He likes to live in the capital, as you know. They even say that when Sigurd is there, the cabarets never close!

OLAF: Yes, so I've heard. But Sigurd is like that — warm-hearted, lively, always in good spirits. He likes to be well-known.

HELENA: His uncles have invited me to Christiania next month for the horse show. Sigurd's taking part.

OLAF: How long does it last?

HELENA: Almost the whole month.

OLAF: As long as that! Will you go?

HELENA: I don't know.

OLAF: Go, Helena. You should see each other more often. You must get used to the idea! Isn't it funny? Although your marriage doesn't concern me personally, I feel so enthusiastic about it — while you, who are directly involved, are still only considering it. We should thank God that your bridegroom isn't some stranger, who would take you away so that we would lose you altogether! But with Sigurd you'll stay here! You *will* invite me sometimes to play dominoes? Don't you think it's funny that I'll be blessing your betrothal? Come now, give me a smile.
(HELENA *bursts into tears.*)
OLAF: Helena (*He looks around anxiously.*) Oh my God, it's just as well no-one is passing.
HELENA: Forgive me. Do you want us to go in?
OLAF: No, no, better stay here. Come, calm yourself.
HELENA: I *will*.
OLAF: Tears aren't good for the eyes, and especially not for beautiful eyes.
HELENA: Don't mock me, Olaf. At school you used to call me "squinty-eyes".
OLAF: But at that time you *were* a little ...
(*He laughs, making* HELENA *laugh too.*)
HELENA: Olaf.
OLAF: Yes, Helena.
HELENA: Perhaps you want to think about it again?
OLAF: Think again? Think about what again?
HELENA: Your, your advice ... I'll come by tomorrow ... or the day after tomorrow?
OLAF: No. Why? My advice will be exactly the same.
HELENA: Are you so sure about what you say?
OLAF: I didn't think it up just now. No, Helena, don't expect me to tell you anything different tomorrow! Years from now I will say the same thing.
HELENA: Very well then, Olaf.
OLAF: And you might *not* get married.
(*She gives him a profoundly questioning look.*)
OLAF: That's your own affair, of course. But don't pressure me into telling you what to decide!
HELENA: I didn't think of pressuring you for one moment. Forgive me if I made you feel like that. I didn't mean to.
OLAF: Marry Sigurd, Helena. It's the best solution.
HELENA: The best solution for whom?

OLAF: For you, naturally! Listen, do you want my general views on marriage? Do you want me to speak more openly?

HELENA: Of course I do. What do I know about it?

OLAF: I don't believe, Helena, that marriage should be an intoxicating romance, a garden of pleasures. Who promised this to you all, that you should expect it? The church doesn't bless marriage, and ordain that "the twain shall be one flesh", simply to give licence for fun and games in the bedroom. It would be a grave error to believe that.

HELENA: What exactly do you mean, Olaf?

OLAF: It's obvious what I mean. It doesn't matter whom you marry. But it *does* matter what you *do* with the man you marry! That's what I mean.

HELENA: What must I do or not do? I don't understand.

OLAF: No, I can't say any more. I've said enough already.

HELENA: We aren't children!

OLAF: Work the rest out for yourself, Helena. After all, I'm not saying anything new! It's well known that most people abuse their marriage — abuse it shamefully! They exploit the divine gift of being able to bear children in order to indulge their licentiousness — they drift into unspeakable orgies!

HELENA: And where did *you* learn this?

OLAF: It's common knowledge. There are even books that describe it, in hair-raising detail.

HELENA: You're frightening me.

OLAF: Why? What have you to do with all that? *You* are Helena. I dared to tell you about these things, because you are chaste and innocent and... and we are such good friends. I have to help you.

HELENA: Yes, Olaf.

OLAF: In any case, all this depends on the woman — *on you*, Helena! The man is the inferior being in this matter! Don't let yourself be carried away by his primal appetites — and become like Sigurd or any other carnivorous playboy! Don't let him have such rights to your body, or you will lose your rights to your soul! I'm not saying don't have children — but when you are both united for that purpose, concentrate your mind on that alone, imploring God to make you conceive! You don't need pleasure! For women, sexual pleasure and procreation are completely unrelated organic functions! The man, on the contrary, functions like an animal! But the woman has no need to be voluptuous in order to give birth, because she is by nature superior. She is a divinity in herself. You said that "you want to be yourself". Marriage will not prevent you from always being yourself, if you want it with all your heart. Everything depends on you, Helena. I'm simply explaining to you how you can preserve your... your superiority! (*A short silence*) Naturally, you mustn't say a word about this to anyone. We two have had such a close relationship since we were children... a communion of souls, I would say. We are young modern people. We can dare to express ourselves more freely sometimes. Besides, these thoughts are private, personal. It's the first time I've expressed them.

HELENA: Thank you, Olaf. I must go now. Would you like these? I gathered them for you. (*She leaves the esparto grass beside him, rises and goes off.*)

NIGHTWATCHMAN (*to* MANDERS *who has remained thoughtful*): My God, what that poor girl had to listen to!

MANDERS: Everything I told her, I believe.

NIGHTWATCHMAN: You said some harsh things, pastor.

MANDERS: Was I less hard on myself?

NIGHTWATCHMAN: No. But you were so young. How could you find it in your heart to say such things!

MANDERS: I had to.

NIGHTWATCHMAN: What a time to choose! You saw fit to say these things to her on the very day she came to you with such love and apprehension.

MANDERS: It was just the right day, don't you understand? Harsh or not, the uncertainty had to come to an end!

NIGHTWATCHMAN: But it didn't come to an end.

MANDERS: I'm not to blame for that! Why are you looking at me like that? Have you some objection?

NIGHTWATCHMAN: With your permission, yes, and a serious one at that.

MANDERS: Listen. You've been thirty years in the theatre but *I've* been forty two, and moreover...

NIGHTWATCHMAN: Pastor, I like you. I respect you, but it's impossible for us to talk if you're going to be like this.

MANDERS: Very well. I take it back! I'm listening to you. I said I'm listening to you.

NIGHTWATCHMAN: Seriously, pastor, were you expecting to put an end to it with that confession of love? I tell you I was suffering!

I've never heard a more dramatic and passionate outburst! I couldn't believe what I was hearing. That you could have been so different even all those years ago — well if I hadn't seen it with my own eyes I just wouldn't have believed it! You were another person!

MANDERS: But we're getting away from the subject.

NIGHTWATCHMAN: No, we're not getting away from it at all. Shall I tell you the mistake you made? She came to find out whether you loved her or not, and trying not to betray yourself you ended up showing that you worship her! What confusion you caused her! Did you think about that?

MANDERS: Wait a minute! How do *you* know exactly what happened.

NIGHTWATCHMAN: I beg your pardon.

MANDERS: And I beg you not to jump to conclusions! Well then, I mustered all my self-control and common sense. I even risked appearing repellent. I sifted everything I said, so that there wouldn't be a trace of personal weakness.

NIGHTWATCHMAN: That's what you think now, but *then* . . .

MANDERS: Please don't interrupt me. I didn't interrupt you.

NIGHTWATCHMAN: You know, pastor, I think it's unnatural — a twenty-something year old man. I'm curious. Will you let me question him?

MANDERS: No! I remember just as well what I felt, and what I did, and what my intention was! If I made a mistake it was in demanding that she be a superior being . . . strong, incorruptible, that she be an exception . . . that she should be what *I* too wanted to be.

NIGHTWATCHMAN: Agh, pastor, I fear you were taking her where *you* wanted her to go.

MANDERS: Is it unreasonable, in this vulgar age, to lead someone to those principles one aspires to oneself?

NIGHTWATCHMAN: It depends. Sometimes we want the other person to be the same as us, because it's easier for us.

MANDERS: Certainly not where I was concerned! I confessed to you that I even wrote poems to her. Do you think it was easy for me to stifle my feelings and devote myself wholeheartedly to my work?

NIGHTWATCHMAN: Ah, your work. That's why you made the decision not to marry?

MANDERS: That's why.

NIGHTWATCHMAN: When did you decide?

MANDERS: When I was at Theological College. There I discovered the value of having the strength to be able to renounce! The strength to deny yourself! And how much you can achieve, thanks to your willingness to deny yourself!

NIGHTWATCHMAN I see! Did the other students make the same decision?

MANDERS: Only one other! I didn't intend to become the typical pastor who gets married, who has children — who can't do anything remarkable.

NIGHTWATCHMAN: I understand. But before that — I mean, what made you decide to become a minister? From what I've seen, you were a strapping young man — the girls liked you.

MANDERS: Ah, my dear friend, the things you're reminding me of.
(*The voice of the other nightwatchman interrupts him.*)

VOICE: What's happening? Have you eaten?

NIGHTWATCHMAN: I can't see you. Where are you?

VOICE: In the balcony.

MANDERS: Tell him to go away. I don't want other people here just now!

NIGHTWATCHMAN: Have you come in here with a cigarette? Are you mad? No smoking in the auditorium — ever!

VOICE: It's only for a minute.

NIGHTWATCHMAN: Not for one minute, not for half a minute!

MANDERS: Don't let him disturb us. What's he doing?

NIGHTWATCHMAN: And stay down please. Stop wandering about. There are some newspapers lying around. Take them and read them. That's right. Good. He's gone. I forgot to ask you — I've a bottle of beer. Would you like me to get a glass and pour you some?

MANDERS: No thanks.

NIGHTWATCHMAN: I've a sandwich too. What do you say?

MANDERS: Maybe later.

NIGHTWATCHMAN: Whenever you like. I'm at your service. Well then?

MANDERS: When did I think of becoming a minister? Isn't that what we were talking about? And you, when did you think of becoming an actor, and why? Think about it! You'll find that there isn't just one reason for taking this road or that road. My first childhood dream was to become a railway stationmaster, then a captain of ships going to Denmark. Afterwards, the church attracted me — or to be precise, the Sunday sermon and the organ — Mrs Alving used to tell me I play the organ very well — the echo in the dome, the stained-glass windows. At that time we had an excellent pastor, a mesmerising speaker. When he went up to the pulpit and began his sermon, everyone became enraptured by him. And he had the voice for it — a deep, solemn voice. It filled the church! Although he was as harsh as a Jewish prophet, they drank in every word of his sermon. They obeyed him. They did whatever he told them.

NIGHTWATCHMAN: Was he married?

MANDERS: He was a widower. After the sermon, he would give the signal for the hymns. I sang in the choir with Helena. They were the most magical moments of my life. I felt I was in paradise. Even now I can sing well.

NIGHTWATCHMAN: I sing a bit too.

MANDERS: And another thing — my father was a leather merchant. Didn't belong to the lower orders, nor to the elite class. Unlike myself, my childhood friends, like Alving, were from old, noble families. Why would they worry if they didn't achieve anything in their lives? Their name and the family fortune alone were enough to make them great and powerful! I won't deny that this played its role, that it was this inequality that motivated me. And I think it's a gift from God, that through the church I found the way to develop my youthful ambitions and talents!

NIGHTWATCHMAN: I understand.

MANDERS: Naturally, miracles don't happen. You try to elevate your soul, but it's a constant uphill struggle. You can't stop being a man. Again and again, you suppress your personal weaknesses — but they have nine lives! And do you know why? Because the weaknesses of others come along to reawaken your own! What would have happened if I hadn't succeeded in suppressing them again on that night! You'd have been sorry for me.

NIGHTWATCHMAN: What night are you talking about, pastor?

MANDERS: *That* night!

NIGHTWATCHMAN: You mean the night she came to you.

MANDERS: Yes, the night she came to me! You were very sorry for Helena just now.

NIGHTWATCHMAN: For both of you.

MANDERS: Especially for her. So don't pretend. It was as clear as daylight you were on her side! Anyhow, you'll learn a lot more.

Provided you have patience, and pay more careful attention!

NIGHTWATCHMAN: I *am* doing that.

MANDERS: Didn't she say that Alving's proposal took her by surprise? Wasn't she hesitating over her decision? Didn't she seem to you very hurt by my attitude? And yet, the following Sunday at the Alvings' house — where indeed they *did* invite me and, as I had expected, I played the piano the whole evening for them to dance — they announced their engagement. Two weeks later, they exchanged rings — I blessed them, and read a celebratory poem that I had written — and four months later, the wedding took place. Such haste and impatience and amnesia. Mind you, I'm not complaining! I mention these things simply as pieces of evidence in the story. The wedding ceremony, magnificent of course, took place in Christiania Cathedral. For the honeymoon, they travelled to Italy. They went as far as Capri. I mustn't forget one detail: when they returned they didn't invite me . . . Helena explained that her aunts, who had undertaken to send the invitations, had made many similar blunders.

NIGHTWATCHMAN: Did that upset you very much?

MANDERS: Yes, it upset me. Even though I wasn't sure if I would go. They had invited, only from Christiania, about four hundred people. Who would have cared whether I was there or not? And there was the expense. But let me tell you about the night when Mrs Alving alleged that I had committed a crime! Because she had fled from her husband she came to my house without warning. She was raving, "I'm yours, I'm yours" — and God gave me the strength to persuade her to return to her husband! How could I ever have become her partner and accomplice in this flighty behaviour? . . . Granted, she was young then, immature — you saw for yourself, she was volatile; one week she'd do one thing, and the next, something quite different. But is it fair that she should call me to account now, at *her* age, and for the stalls, the balcony, the gallery to hear her, and look on her as my victim? However, to set the record straight, once and for all, this is what happened. It was barely one and a half years since the day of their wedding. It was a Saturday, just after nine o'clock at night, and I was writing my Sunday sermon. She chose the right moment, as you see.

(OLAF *comes on stage, looking towards the door where someone is knocking persistently. Anxiously, he goes over and opens it.*

HELENA *bursts in. She looks overwrought, tormented.* OLAF *stands at the door, disconcerted, uneasy, looking first at* HELENA *and then outside.*)

MANDERS: I thought I was dreaming. What did she want here at this hour? The wind was howling outside. Helena looked distressed, frightened, wild.

HELENA: Why are you standing at the door?

OLAF: Who else is out there?

HELENA: Nobody.

OLAF: Did you come alone?

HELENA: Yes.

OLAF: At this hour?

HELENA: I wasn't in a state to think about the time.

OLAF: What's the matter? What's happened?

HELENA: Calm yourself, Olaf. I haven't come to eat you.

OLAF: In Heaven's name, this is no time for jokes!

HELENA: When you hear the reason I've come, you'll forgive me for alarming you.

OLAF: No, you're not alarming me, only . . .

HELENA: Then come, sit down and listen to me.

OLAF: Of course. Shall I tell her to bring you some tea?

HELENA: Who?

OLAF: Eve, my housekeeper.

HELENA: No, I'd like you just to close that door.

OLAF: There's no need. She can't hear us. She sleeps up in the attic.

HELENA: I'd feel better if it were closed.

OLAF: But if she comes down by chance and sees it closed, it's not unlikely that she'll listen. You know what old women are like.

HELENA (*overcome with anxiety and shattered nerves*): Will you stop being afraid of your own shadow, Pastor Manders!

OLAF (*offended*): Me? Afraid? You think it's fear. (*He goes and closes the door with an ostentatious movement.*) There you are! Is there anything else I can do to prevent you calling me a coward? Silly girl! It's you I want to protect!

HELENA: I don't need protection! I only wanted the door closed so that we could have some privacy.

OLAF: All right then, let's say that we have.
(*They look each other straight in the eye for a moment without speaking.*)

HELENA (*embraces him, giving vent to her feelings*): Help, Olaf,

help! Hold me please! Hold me!
(*Taken aback,* OLAF *submits to her embrace and, lost in submission, embraces her too.*)
OLAF: What's happening to you, Helena? What's happening?
HELENA: I've left home, Olaf!
(OLAF *draws back from her and looks her in the eyes trying to understand.*)
OLAF: You've left!
HELENA: I don't want to go back!
OLAF: And you came here.
HELENA: To you, Olaf! Who else would I come to!
OLAF: Yes, of course... you did right. But compose yourself and... yes... and what exactly is happening?
HELENA: You don't know?
OLAF: How would *I* know? Why *should* I know?
HELENA: All this time you've heard nothing? You know nothing?
OLAF: Helena, you know very well that all this time I've been devoting myself heart and soul to my work. I've begun a long-term programme. I haven't any spare time for... and besides, I don't take for gospel what this one and that one says.
HELENA: But you've been to our house four times. Didn't you notice anything at all?
OLAF: I wasn't coming to your house to see whether you were both happy or not! I was coming on other business, like the...
HELENA: How many times did you find Alving at home?
OLAF: I didn't think it strange, since his business is chiefly in Christiania.
HELENA: His mistresses and his amusements are in Christiania! And at home, I'm nothing more than a mistress to him.
OLAF: You didn't say a word to me.
HELENA: I was ashamed... and whenever I saw you, I felt so happy that I didn't want to spoil it all with my complaints. But I can't take any more!
OLAF: So, he hasn't changed.
HELENA: I couldn't care less that he's deceiving me with the cabaret dancers. But I can't endure feeling ridiculous, and thinking what a farce my grand wedding was, with all the advice, the festivities, and everyone's good wishes.
OLAF: Helena, my dear, I'm listening to you with love and understanding, but it isn't right to think that others are to blame! And besides, are you sure you're not exaggerating?

HELENA: Olaf, you haven't heard anything yet!

OLAF: How often . . . How much is he at home?

HELENA: Whenever he feels like it! But even when he *is* at home what state do you think he's in? He starts drinking first thing in the morning. By midday he doesn't know where he is. In the evening, he gathers all his drinking friends together. They drink like animals. They play cards and assault the housemaids. They don't even respect me. They leer at me. Once, I had to slap one of them on the face when he grabbed my hand and licked it! I lock myself in my room. I cover my ears and cry. When they leave at daybreak, the house stinks like a tavern! When I do find a rare opportunity to speak to him, he bows his head like a naughty child, and promises to mend his ways. But the next day, he does the same thing again. The worst of it is I'm slowly beginning to get used to living in this quagmire. I'm slowly beginning to lose myself! And when I become aware of it, like this evening, I'm seized with panic! I can see that the longer I stay, the more trapped I become. That if I don't leave now, I'll never leave!

(*A silence.* HELENA *looks at* OLAF, *waiting in anguish for his response.*)

OLAF: Need I tell you how sorry I am? Oh God, how difficult it all is! What strange ground are we treading! But of course I'll help you. I want to with all my heart. It is my duty to help you! But one of us has to see the whole situation more coolly.

HELENA (*almost crying out*): Don't send me back, I beg you!

OLAF: Did I suggest such a thing? Before we thought it over? Do you think I'm so shallow?

HELENA: I'm sorry.

OLAF: In any case, for you to get up and leave, isn't perhaps the only solution. Or the best. Maybe you should discuss it with your mother and your aunts? Besides, several opinions are better than one. Why rely on my opinion only? What experience do I have?

HELENA: I know what they'll say to me!

OLAF: Why would they say anything harmful? They worship you.

HELENA: They'll tell me I'm not the first, nor will I be the last — that I'm having difficulties in adjusting, that I should return to Alving, and strive with patience and persistence to reform him, because Sigurd is really a good soul. And when I find his weak spot I'll be able to mould him by example.

OLAF: And is this anything to be ironic about? I don't understand you. Do you think I would suggest something different? Why would I? I love you more than to do that, and I know all about the frictions between young couples before they get used to each other. Even so, I would advise something else. Leave him, but don't be hasty. You don't have to decide this evening! Don't go back to Alving now. Go back tomorrow morning. Find an excuse to sleep at your mother's house tonight. Then you'll have time to think it over, and discuss it again more calmly. This wind is terrible. One can't concentrate.

(*A silence.*)

HELENA: Do you remember how you wanted to be a stationmaster? You even had a whistle. Do you still have it? *You* were the stationmaster. Alving, myself and the other children were the passengers. What a prophetic game that was. Now it feels like I *have* ended up in a train and I don't know where it's going. Either it hasn't got an emergency handle, or the handle's broken. I can't stop the train and get out. The engine driver doesn't know anything about this, nor does he care if he's hauling a passenger who didn't want to go with them in the first place.

OLAF: What does this parable mean? Speak clearly. You believe I've harmed you?

HELENA: No, since you didn't do it on purpose. Nor could you have imagined what road it would take me down.

OLAF: You're being obscure again. What exactly are you referring to now?

HELENA: To your instructions concerning the marital bed. It isn't just as simple as you think. You're woefully inexperienced — tragically ignorant.

OLAF: Inexperienced yes, but I had tormented myself thinking about it all.

HELENA: And I'm telling you from my tormented experience, Olaf, that no matter what a brute the man you're sleeping with is, it's impossible to be constantly impassive and aloof. No-one's made of stone.

OLAF: What do you mean? That sometimes you happened to get carried away?

HELENA: Not sometimes, many times! And it didn't just happen. I wanted to be carried away!

OLAF: That is utterly impossible!

HELENA: Do you prefer your self-deceiving fantasies?

OLAF: I thought you were different from other women. I thought you were strong!
HELENA: I thought so too. That's why I believed you!
OLAF: Then I was deceived!
HELENA: I didn't deceive you!
OLAF: Then who did?
HELENA (*aggressively but in distress*): Have you ever been in bed with a naked woman?
OLAF: In the name of Heaven, what kind of talk is this?
HELENA: Why not this kind of talk? Because if you answer me honestly, it might not be so easy for you to say that I deceived you? Speak as I do. Have you ever found yourself in bed with a naked woman, who may be an animal, but a beautiful animal for all that? Even if you *have* so little experience, don't look so shocked! And if you have none at all, don't make a god out of your ignorance!
OLAF: Is it fitting that you should bring me down to your level? I am a minister of the church, Helena! I give an account of my experiences and mistakes elsewhere! And in any case, why say all this? Where's it taking you?
HELENA: Nowhere, Olaf. I know now that fine words have no body. Have your opinions if you must, but don't deceive future admirers and have *them* on your conscience! Not once did I make advances to him, but when he began to rub his body against mine, to caress me, to kiss me, there were times when I managed to distance myself. But there were so many other times when I only pretended to resist. He thought he was raping me, but hypocrite that I was, I enjoyed the rape.
OLAF: Stop.
HELENA: Your instructions developed into a method of perversion.
OLAF: I can see that, and it breaks my heart! Only a corrupt woman would be able to utter, with such cynicism, the things that you're saying now!
HELENA: And yet I swear to you that only at those times do I not know what I'm doing and who I am. Afterwards I think only of you and I loathe myself. I'm afraid to look at myself in the mirror. My face is no longer mine. It has the shadow of vulgarity on it. I hate him! It's the first time in my life I've felt hate. I caught myself thinking that if he happened to be killed in a hunting accident I'd . . .
OLAF: That's enough!! Helena, Helena, what am I hearing from

you!

HELENA: Save me Olaf. (*She falls to her knees and embraces his feet, clasping them.*) I'm yours. I've always been yours, only yours!

OLAF (*looking lost, trapped*): Think what you're saying!

HELENA: Yes, Olaf, I'm yours. Take me. Save me . . .

OLAF: What can *I* do?

HELENA: Everything. You only have to want to.

OLAF: No, no!

HELENA: I beg you. Feel like a young man. Be a young man! Why do you insist on denying life? Other ministers get married, have a family. Why do *you* choose to die so young? Can't you understand that I should belong to you and you to me? Come out of your tomb! We'll be happy, I swear to you. I'll be the woman you want, just as *you* want her. (*She stops, exhausted. She takes her hands away from his feet. Without raising her head to look him in the face, she realises that she has no hope.*) Say something. Whatever it is. It's worse when you don't speak. I feel much more lonely now that I've told you everything.

OLAF: What else can I say? I'm sorry, Helena. I've said whatever I had to say.

(HELENA *now raises her eyes and sees him standing expressionless, motionless, master of the situation.*)

HELENA: *When . . . ?*

OLAF Before. Even before I heard everything.

HELENA (*wryly*): And now that you've heard everything? (*She gets up wearily and goes towards the door.*)

OLAF: I'll go with you as far as . . .

HELENA: No, pastor, thank you. I'm not afraid of the night or the storm.

(*The* NIGHTWATCHMAN, *totally absorbed by the scene, follows her to the door. He stands there watching her go away.*)

MANDERS: Isn't it sad?

(*The* NIGHTWATCHMAN *closes the door and comes back, looking fixedly at* OLAF.)

MANDERS: I used to call her the smile of the Virgin, a snowflake on the branches of the willow.

OLAF: A ray of sunlight in the fountain.

MANDERS: Yes!

NIGHTWATCHMAN (*to* OLAF): She left in a wretched state.

OLAF: I could see that.

MANDERS: She came in a wretched state!
NIGHTWATCHMAN: But she left in a worse one, pastor!
OLAF: That's why I suggested accompanying her.
MANDERS: She was very wrong to come in the first place!
NIGHTWATCHMAN: Why don't you let him speak?
MANDERS: Because I've thought about it a thousand times and the result is always the same!
NIGHTWATCHMAN: Yes, but she explained why she came, more than she needed to.
MANDERS: If she'd had the strength to exercise control over herself, she wouldn't have needed to come in the middle of the night to explain!
NIGHTWATCHMAN: But, pastor, can we always do as we should?
MANDERS: So you weren't horrified by what you heard?
NIGHTWATCHMAN: Yes, pastor, but by everything — not just the half of it. And for that reason, I haven't the heart to judge her.
MANDERS: But it suits you to judge me.
NIGHTWATCHMAN: Not at all, I swear to you.
MANDERS: Nevertheless, you're allowing yourself to be carried away. You're biased.
NIGHTWATCHMAN: After thirty years in the theatre don't tell me I'm biased! You offend me!
MANDERS: Perhaps you suspect I'm not telling you what really happened?
NIGHTWATCHMAN: On the contrary, pastor.
MANDERS: I would never have done that! Do you think that as the third party in this story, it didn't torture me to see what happened?
NIGHTWATCHMAN: Don't I see that it tortures you? You move me more than you can imagine. I mean that! But here's the curious thing in this affair: that while you present it all, so objectively . . .
OLAF: Don't torment me. What else could I do? Destroy my career before it had even begun? Yield to a woman's blackmail, and say the same things as she was saying to me?
NIGHTWATCHMAN: What blackmail?
OLAF: "I'm yours, I'm yours."
NIGHTWATCHMAN: You're wrong. Blackmail wouldn't be heartrending like that.
OLAF: Wasn't she leading me into a tragic impasse? I didn't know what to say, or what to do. I was trembling for fear she would

get up and kiss me on the mouth.
NIGHTWATCHMAN: Yes, but she didn't get up, nor did she kiss you on the mouth. (*To the older* MANDERS): So, pastor . . .
MANDERS: Don't look at me, at my age. Keep to this young man's problem!
NIGHTWATCHMAN: Yes, of course. But she was young too!
MANDERS: She was young, but with eighteen months' experience of marriage — and you even heard how skilfully she acquired it.
NIGHTWATCHMAN: Well, if she had come to beguile you, she'd have put on make-up. She'd have dressed up. She wouldn't have come looking so pitiful!
OLAF: It was Helena, and that was enough.
MANDERS: And besides, I know many pitiful women who are much more attractive than many happy ones.
NIGHTWATCHMAN: What can I say? I'm confused now too.
MANDERS: Don't make the mistake of comparing Helena before she got married to the Helena of that night. There is no comparison.
OLAF: The pity of it.
MANDERS: She was a different person. She said so herself. She saw it in her mirror.
OLAF: I wanted to cover my ears against her. I thought it was a prostitute from the docks talking. Dear God, how could she *think* of coming here, and bringing everything about her marriage bed out into the open!
NIGHTWATCHMAN: But why did she do it? A girl doesn't humiliate herself like that if she isn't very moral. I know something about women.
MANDERS: Moral?
NIGHTWATCHMAN: Wasn't it innocence that made her come and tell you the whole story?
MANDERS: And tell me about her perversions?
NIGHTWATCHMAN: But the girl believed you. She adored you, and the . . . the . . . the beautiful and noble thing is that she came to tell you.
MANDERS: Why did she want to grieve *me*!
OLAF: I'm not made of stone either.
MANDERS: She wanted to revenge herself on me, and she succeeded.
NIGHTWATCHMAN: Who would come to take revenge and say, "Help me. Help me."

OLAF: She broke my heart! Suppose I had lost my head and given way! How could I see her again, a besmirched woman, as a snowflake and the smile of the Virgin? From that night, the only picture I had of her was naked in Alving's bed, being violated . . . and secretly enjoying it, looking at me with half-closed eyes.

NIGHTWATCHMAN: Seriously?

OLAF: For years! I prayed I'd grow old quickly and perhaps find some peace with myself.

NIGHTWATCHMAN: So she hadn't stopped hurting you.

MANDERS: I'll confess something to you that only God knows. I'll reveal it to you alone to assure you how sincere I am. When they got married I wept. And worse — I didn't wish them ill — but deep down in my heart I really didn't want them to be happy.

OLAF: Then I burned all our souvenirs — letters from the time I was at college in Christiania, and all the poems I had written to her. I gathered the ashes and kept them in a biscuit tin.

MANDERS: It's still in some drawer.

NIGHTWATCHMAN: Good grief! What am I hearing this evening? At the end of the day, pastor, we know very little about anything. And then what happened?

MANDERS: Let's leave the personal aspect out of it for a moment, because this matter didn't begin and end with her and myself. Can you imagine the public scandal that would have broken out? "Young pastor lives with runaway bride!"

NIGHTWATCHMAN: Terrible! And they say it takes bal — I do beg your pardon — I mean it takes guts to face that!

MANDERS: That's as may be. But why? To play the man? Look what Mrs Alving charged me with. She considers me a coward because I sent her back, instead of burdening myself with her and the failure of her marriage! But in the end was I or was I not my own master?

OLAF: Don't forget that, especially after their marriage, I stayed aloof and devoted myself to my work. The congregation was inspired by my sermons. I wrote new hymns and set them to music. Everyone began to take note of me. The bishop was informed of the innovative philanthropic programme I was preparing, and wanted to meet me. The Stavanger journal, *The Ten Commandments*, commissioned a series of articles from me. All the best families in Rosenvold invited me to their table on Sunday. I was already quite a name.

MANDERS: Paid for with the sacrifice of my virile body and youthful heart! Yes, indeed, Mrs Alving! And it still rankles with you that I didn't destroy young pastor Manders in order to gratify the follies of your temperament! (*To the* NIGHTWATCHMAN): For me that woman was deadly. It was as if she'd made a vow to shatter my integrity, and anything in my actions that was incompatible with her desires! The integrity that I've been struggling, through self-denial, to hold on to my whole life. What you are about to see took place twenty five years later. Pay particular attention to her strategy!

(OLAF *moves away to one side and listens.*)

MANDERS: I had received a letter from her, in which she requested that we meet to discuss an interesting matter. I replied that I was at her disposal. I should mention that poor Alving had died eight years earlier, of cirrhosis of the liver — (it was I who buried him). I was glad that I would see her again, although it was the height of naivety to assume that the older Mrs Alving was now harmless. Don't forget that after that terrible night, our relations were entirely formal. We saw each other rarely, and never alone. I believe we — and especially she — had finally accepted that there was no question of our being more than old acquaintances. Years ago, without realising it, I slipped into the plural form when I spoke to her. And she did the same. I believed that she, like myself, would consider the formal mode of address a wise move — it created a salutary coolness, a safe distance between us. And I had every reason to believe it, because for twenty-five years, one never said to the other, "Do you remember this or that" — something I was in dread of. But not a thing! Not the slightest thing! It was as if we were suffering from amnesia. But at this meeting, I had to deal again with a different person. (*The older Helena,* MRS ALVING, *comes on stage.*) It was many years since I had been in her house. Except for her, nothing else had changed.

MRS ALVING: Come in, pastor.

MANDERS: Good evening, Mrs Alving.

(*They shake hands.*)

MRS ALVING: I'm glad to see you.

MANDERS: Likewise.

MRS ALVING: Are you well?

MANDERS: I am, thank God. And you?

MRS ALVING: Well.

MANDERS: It's nice to see the weather has improved.
MRS ALVING: It is nice. We even saw a little of the sun today.
MANDERS: Have you heard from Osvald, Mrs Alving? Is he well?
MRS ALVING: He's very well pastor, thank you. I had a letter from him the day before yesterday! Ah my darling boy writes to me so often.
MANDERS: Is he still over in Paris?
MRS ALVING: Still. Paris is the ideal place for a young man.
MANDERS: So I've heard.
MRS ALVING: Where would you like to sit?
MANDERS: Oh, anywhere at all.
MRS ALVING: Sit here then.
MANDERS: Thank you.
MRS ALVING: What can we offer you?
MANDERS: Perhaps I might ask for a cup of tea later.
MRS ALVING: As you wish. First of all, pastor, I want to thank you, with all my heart, for having the goodness to come.
MANDERS: Don't mention it, Mrs Alving.
MRS ALVING: I imagine your time is precious.
MANDERS: It's no trouble, I assure you. Besides, you said in your letter that it was about a very interesting matter.
MRS ALVING: So I think. Ah! By the way I must congratulate you on your new post!
MANDERS: New post?
MRS ALVING: I read about it in the papers!
MANDERS: You mean the Theological College? Thank you, Mrs Alving. But it's not really a post. The title of "doctor" is an honorary one.
MRS ALVING: But it is higher than professor.
MANDERS: Don't worry about it. I don't attach much importance to these things.
MRS ALVING: In any case, we're very pleased. It's an honour for all of Rosenvold.
MANDERS: You're too kind, Mrs Alving.
MRS ALVING: And you deserve it. From what I know you work very hard.
MANDERS: Each according to his strength.
MRS ALVING: But let's not waste your time. Let's get to the point.
MANDERS: I'm all ears.
MRS ALVING: Pastor, I thought of establishing a home for orphans, or for poor children generally.

MANDERS: Mrs Alving!!
MRS ALVING: Excuse me?
MANDERS: Nothing. I'm sorry. Go on!
MRS ALVING: A house, where these children will have a roof over their heads, good food, warm clothing, teachers, and loving care.
MANDERS: Mrs Alving, I'm sincerely moved, and I congratulate you from the bottom of my heart.
MRS ALVING: I have secured all the necessary funds for it to function unimpeded, without support from elsewhere.
MANDERS: Bravo!
MRS ALVING: And it will be called "The Captain Sigurd Alving Memorial Children's Home."
(MANDERS *is clearly taken aback by this last remark.*)
MRS ALVING: Since I don't know what documents are necessary and what action I must take to get permission etc. etc., I'm asking you to help me. You have great experience in such matters.
MANDERS (*feeling embarrassed*): Yes, I have some experience.
MRS ALVING: You're a councillor for quite similar institutions, are you not?
MANDERS: Yes *of course* I am.
MRS ALVING: Are the procedures simple or . . . ? How exactly does one begin? How does one start?
MANDERS: I'll tell you.
MRS ALVING: My solicitor, in any case, is willing to undertake negotiations with the different departments. So what do you say?
MANDERS (*hesitatingly*): Marvellous, yes, indeed . . . but why don't you choose another name?
MRS ALVING: Another name?
MANDERS: There are so many saints, male and female.
MRS ALVING: Why?
MANDERS: Such names would be more suitable.
MRS ALVING: It must be the one I've told you — "The Captain Sigurd Alving Memorial Children's Home". Besides, it will be financed by the estate of the deceased, which will be disposed of entirely for this purpose. As you can see, this is one more reason for choosing the name of the deceased.
MANDERS: The other reason — what is it?
MRS ALVING: May I confide in you?
MANDERS: You're putting me in a difficult position yet again.
MRS ALVING: I'm not forcing you to listen, pastor. I'm asking you

first.

MANDERS (*thinks about it*): Has it any relation to the past?

MRS ALVING: Naturally it relates to the past. Do you think it relates to something that happened on the moon?

MANDERS: All right, tell me, but please let's not digress.

MRS ALVING: I don't want my son to have anything whatsoever to do with his father's estate.

MANDERS: You say that as if you're referring to something vile!

MRS ALVING: The story of my whole life with Alving is vile, and I'm doing whatever I can to clean it up — and more especially my son's life. I don't want him to inherit anything from the deceased.

MANDERS: I thought that after . . . (*He stops.*)

MRS ALVING: Yes?

MANDERS: Nothing! Besides, I was the one who said we shouldn't digress.

MRS ALVING: Oh, come now, pastor. Anyway, what have you to fear now? What was to happen, happened.

MANDERS: So be it, but I'll confine myself to this point! I believed that after you returned to your home on that . . .

MRS ALVING: That night, pastor.

MANDERS: I believed you had found a *modus vivendi*.

MRS ALVING: I don't know any Latin.

MANDERS: A way of living in harmony together!

MRS ALVING: It was three times worse! A real hell!

MANDERS: I can't believe it! Neither myself nor anyone else saw anything wrong.

MRS ALVING: I'm glad to hear it. It means that I succeeded one hundred percent! It's your turn to congratulate *me*. Don't look at me like that. I'm not joking. It was my life's work! That night, I gave you some idea of my life here. But from that time on, I managed not to let the slightest thing leak out. And I paid dearly for it. I deprived myself of my child by sending him, from the age of seven, to a boarding school, and then to Switzerland, and after that, to Paris. But it was out of the question to let Osvald grow up with two monsters — one of them, myself.

(*A pause.*)

MANDERS: I'm so deeply sorry.

MRS ALVING: It would have been devastating for Osvald, who was always very sensitive, to have seen what his father had been reduced to. The lies I wrote to him, the eulogies about his papa!

Do you understand, pastor, how important it is for me that this institution should bear his name? It confirms the perception of his father that I have created in Osvald!

MANDERS: Yes but — pardon me, Mrs Alving — you have created with lies. You've just said so yourself!

MRS ALVING: Does this bother you personally, pastor?

MANDERS: Certainly not, if it remains a family matter! But consider the contaminated estate of the deceased — as you yourself have referred to it — and your abhorrence of him. Wanting to convert it into a philanthropic institution, finding favour in the eyes of God, is — Heaven forfend — a wicked thought!

MRS ALVING: While we're on the subject of wickedness, pastor . . . We said we wouldn't digress, otherwise I could remind you that if I were in the slightest bit wicked, I wouldn't have let my life, and the little happiness apportioned to each of us, slip through my fingers like sand.

MANDERS: Let's confine ourselves to the subject of the orphanage, Mrs Alving! Remember please, what you yourself told me about the dissolute, depraved life of the deceased. Realise *what* you are about to commemorate with this Captain Sigurd Alving Memorial Orphanage! How *could* you have the heart to deceive a whole community?

MRS ALVING: Pastor, the world is ignorant. Have you forgotten what happened at his funeral? The homage. The grief. It was as impressive as our wedding. Do you know that they still talk about the oration you delivered?

MANDERS: Mrs Alving, I did that as a minister at a funeral service, as an official of our holy church and it is the prerogative of the church to forgive. But this institution in his name — you're not doing it to forgive him, or to redeem him. You're doing it to punish him. It would be nothing less than an abominable, despicable fraud, making a mockery of everyone and everything. Of course I'm not saying that you would intend all this — I simply want to impress upon you where your action could lead, without your realising it!

MRS ALVING: Pastor, don't try to dissuade me. I will, no matter what, free myself of the curse of Alving. And the disposal of his estate on such an institution is a decision — if you'll allow me to say so — that finds favour in the eyes of God. The name, which so annoys you, isn't the only dubiously ascribed name in

Rosenvold — or in Norway. Another one won't be the end of the world. I know how happy it will make Osvald, and how proud he'll be of his father. This alone is reason enough. And besides, pastor, it's years since I've chosen to act on my own ideas, no matter how wrong they might be — rather than stitching my life together with old ideas and prejudices — leftovers from other people's lives.

MANDERS: Mrs Alving, to be frank, I don't understand why you invited me, since you obviously have no need of me.

MRS ALVING: You're wrong, pastor.

MANDERS: Why wrong, since you have rejected all my advice. I assure you this is the first time it has ever happened to me!

MRS ALVING: Come now, don't be angry with me. We'll find a way. You know very well that I can't proceed without your help.

MANDERS: Mrs Alving, I'm going to say one or two things that can't be disputed. In the first place, you have again confessed things to me that I should have preferred not to know about! Despite all that, I'll turn a blind eye; I'll overlook your reasons for building this orphanage. But I am unyielding on the question of the name! No, Mrs Alving, that's going beyond the limit! If you persist in wanting this name, don't count on me!

MRS ALVING: I do persist.

MANDERS: I'm sorry, but in that case I don't want any involvement in it!

MRS ALVING: And what shall we say to people?

MANDERS: Don't for Heaven's sake. Don't start blackmailing me.

MRS ALVING: But I haven't put a revolver to your back!

MANDERS: Haven't you?

MRS ALVING: Pastor, you've been blackmailing yourself all your life.

MANDERS: Just what do you mean by that?

MRS ALVING: Pastor, why do you get annoyed by everything I say? You ask me what I mean. Don't you take into account first and foremost what people will say? Why don't you want to admit it? Who are you afraid of?

MANDERS: I fear absolutely no-one!

MRS ALVING: But a moment ago, you were speaking with fear and trepidation about these people. And I assure you, pastor, that I too take them into account when I need them. If I tell you that our meeting today is because of them, how will it seem to you? The first comment of those I spoke to about the Alving

Orphanage was that I should have recourse to you. None of them could contemplate such an institution being created without you as the guiding spirit. As you see, pastor, I could say it wasn't I who chose you for the important role you have to play in the orphanage. You were chosen because of the esteem and respect that everyone has for you. I think you ought to take this very seriously into consideration — as I have done! Think what would happen if I were to say to them: "No, I don't want Manders involved in the institution in any way" or, if I were obliged to say to them that Manders categorically refuses to have any involvement in it. God knows where their minds would run! We'd be the talk of the whole country! They'd begin to look for the reason, to search, to dig. And you know how talented they are at scandal-mongering! Indeed, the more they esteem the person they're gossiping about, the more they're seized with a passion to expose them. I think, pastor, that we're condemned to work together. So let's make this collaboration as harmonious as possible. If however, you continue to reject it, we must find a convincing excuse. Or rather — *you* must! You manage these things better.

MANDERS (*irritated, feeling he's been driven into a corner*): Don't be so hasty, please, Mrs Alving! Don't be so hasty!

MRS ALVING: I'm not being hasty. Think about it at your leisure.

MANDERS: Anyway I've been listening to you all this time and I don't know whether you're being serious or joking!

MRS ALVING: Would I joke about something that pains me? Don't mistake the irony of fate for my cunning. And when all's said and done, can you really tell which of us fate is mocking?

MANDERS: Mrs Alving, have you spoken to many people about the institution?

MRS ALVING: No, about ten at most . . . perhaps twelve.

MANDERS: And you think twelve people aren't many? You couldn't have told me about it first?

MRS ALVING: Pastor, I did it for your own good. I found out first of all how the idea seemed to others, and then, when I was sure about it, I approached you.

MANDERS: And what role do you want me to play in your institution? What exactly have you in mind?

MRS ALVING: Choose it yourself, pastor. But if you don't mind my saying, you cannot be subordinate to others. You must be either president of the board or honorary president!

MANDERS: Are you day-dreaming?

MRS ALVING: On the contrary! I'm trying to see it as anyone would. It'll be the biggest and most perfect institution of its kind in the area, and you're our great name in this field. With all your experience, what would everyone think if it weren't under your patronage? And let's not forget something else: they all know that Alving was your dear childhood friend — you said so at his funeral. Isn't that all the more reason why you should be involved with an institution dedicated to his memory?

MANDERS: What are you forcing me to do!!!

MRS ALVING: *I'm* not forcing you. We've come to this point together, step by step, hand in hand, just putting the seal on something that has crept up on us. That's sincerely how I feel, Olaf.

(MANDERS *wanders thoughtfully back and forth.* MRS ALVING *and* OLAF *leave the stage.*)

MANDERS: You heard. She may not even once have used the phrase "You remember", but she based everything she said on that broad and deep "You remember". And she called me plain "Olaf", as in the past.

NIGHTWATCHMAN: Indeed.

MANDERS: May I have another cigarette?

NIGHTWATCHMAN: I told you — as many as you like. (*He offers the packet.*) I've got hot coffee too. Shall I pour you some?

MANDERS: No thanks. It keeps me awake.

NIGHTWATCHMAN: You're upset again, aren't you?

MANDERS: Very, and I'm not young anymore!

NIGHTWATCHMAN: Rightly so, this time.

MANDERS: Was that blackmail or wasn't it?

NIGHTWATCHMAN: Was it ever! Everything calculated to a hairsbreadth. Not an ounce of spontaneity! Bravo, Mrs Alving!

MANDERS: So I ask you, as the honest man I could swear you are: What would *you* have done in my place?

NIGHTWATCHMAN: Let's face it — I'd have done the same, pastor!

MANDERS (*aggravated*): Of course! And yet a distinguished critic went and wrote, "In the role of the villain Manders, Mister So-and-so was excellent," etcetera! "In the role of the villain!" I sacrificed my whole life for public morality, for the common good, and in the end, I'm called a "villain". But what can I do? How can I defend myself? Sit down and write to him that at least three times in my relations with Mrs Alving, I almost had a *heart attack.*

NIGHTWATCHMAN: Don't attach so much importance to it all. No-one's perfect.

MANDERS: Yes, but I suffer. The others simply judge!

NIGHTWATCHMAN: We'll all be judged one day. You know that. You're a minister!

MANDERS: Then why don't they wait for this judgement? Why must *I* especially, be judged by all and sundry?

NIGHTWATCHMAN: That's the theatre. What can we do? Abolish it? And don't take it personally. Do you know how many have found justice in here? Here, where we're standing! Have patience, pastor. Think about it! I see you differently already. Come, don't let it worry you. Let's go on.

MANDERS: Needless to say, it became quickly known that I had undertaken to be president of the institution. And for one and a half years, everyone who met me felt compelled to ask, "How is Mrs Alving's orphanage coming along? When'll it be ready?" It was purgatory. In any event, it was ready to open in a year and a half. Osvald came home from Paris for the Opening Day, and Mrs Alving was all happiness. She was even saying that perhaps Osvald would stay at home with her for good. (*Thoughtfully*): And in fact he did stay. On the day before the Opening, we met to settle some matters that were pending, and to dine together. Until that moment, or rather until the following day, everything was going according to plan. Or, almost according to plan. At some time in the afternoon, I went out to take a stroll in the grounds, and near where the forest begins I met Osvald. Remember that since he had always been away, I didn't actually know him. Apart from the conversation we had at midday, in the house — and which had been merely cordial — it was the second time we had spoken to each other.

(OSVALD *comes on stage.*)

OSVALD: You like it out here as well?

MANDERS: Ah, yes, very much. Nature, Osvald, nature has inexhaustible beauty.

OSVALD: Betrayed nature.

MANDERS: Yes, you're right. Quite often we treat her dreadfully.

OSVALD: Beginning with ourselves. Everything nestles within us.

MANDERS: Too true, Osvald, too true. Yet, when he wants to, man can adorn divine creation with his own works. Take for example, the Orphanage — how beautiful it looks from here. I hadn't noticed before — isn't it a wonderful idea? An example to be imitated. Have you been to see it, Osvald?

OSVALD: From the moment I arrived, my mother couldn't wait for me to admire it.

MANDERS: Do you like its architecture?

OSVALD: Yes, very much.

MANDERS: It's turned out well, thank God! Did you go inside? Did you see how airy and pleasant the rooms are — the dining-room, the classroom? We considered everything very thoroughly, so that it would be a model of its kind! We were all very enthusiastic about it. And so we should be. An institution in memory of your father had to be worthy of him. Besides, your mother kept telling us over and over: "I want my son to see it and be proud." (*He gives a satisfied laugh.*)

OSVALD: Thank you for your help, pastor!

MANDERS: It was both my pleasure and my duty. So many things bind us together!

OSVALD: By the way, pastor, how well did you know my father?

MANDERS: How well? We were friends, remember, since childhood!

OSVALD: Unfortunately, I knew him very little. He died so young.

MANDERS: You were at school abroad of course! You see, he had great ambitions for you!

OSVALD: But was it right, in the name of ambitions for my future, to deprive me of their company so much?

MANDERS: You think they didn't want you to be with them? Your studies, however, were of prime importance.

OSVALD: In the end, I grew up an orphan. Do you think that's why the Orphanage has been founded? In memory of the orphan, Osvald? (*He laughs.*)

MANDERS (*putting on a smile*): Don't ever say that to your mother. She won't laugh at all.

OSVALD: Of course not.

MANDERS: But, Osvald, from the conversation we had this afternoon, I understood that you liked being abroad.

OSVALD: Not when I was a child, pastor. I suffered then.

MANDERS: Did you tell them?

OSVALD: No.

MANDERS: Why not?

OSVALD: Because I'd got the idea into my head that they didn't want me here, that they had banished me!

MANDERS: If you knew how wrong you were!
OSVALD: Are you sure?
MANDERS: Would I speak to you like this if I weren't?
OSVALD: I have this permanent feeling that I've never known my parents, that I really don't know who they are.
MANDERS: It's because you were away.
OSVALD: It's not only that.
MANDERS: What then?
OSVALD: Something even more serious ... and it creates a void in me — a wasting grief.
MANDERS: I think you need to live for a while with your mother and the spirit of your father.
OSVALD: I'd like that, but there's a complication. Inevitably, I'd have to stay in the same house, in our house. Do you know what I remember most about it? Myself as a child, secretly listening to angry voices, peeping through keyholes at my mother being mauled about, and a maid grabbing me to hurry me out of the house — rain, hail, or snow — and taking me for a walk. Later these walks became school in Switzerland.
MANDERS: I don't know what to say. I'm shocked.
OSVALD: May I ask you a favour?
MANDERS: Of course. But what, Osvald?
OSVALD: That we talk about my parents.
(MANDERS *becomes tense and silent.*)
OSVALD: You're the only one I can ask. However, if you have reasons for not wanting ...
MANDERS (*nervously*): No, Osvald, what reasons would I have?
OSVALD: How should I know?
MANDERS: I was just thinking what a fate mine is. To be for everyone the only one who ...
OSVALD: Isn't that natural?
MANDERS: Yes — but what exactly do you want to discuss, Osvald? Don't imagine I know anything other than what came under my notice.
OSVALD: So be it. I suspect that something was happening between my parents.
MANDERS: Such as?
OSVALD: Did they get on well?
MANDERS: I would say ... normally ... like all married couples.
OSVALD: Did my father drink a lot?
MANDERS: He liked a good wine. But who doesn't like good

French wine!
OSVALD: Perhaps he liked it too much?
MANDERS: Perhaps a little more than is usual.
OSVALD: And did he like women more than is usual?
MANDERS: Listen, Osvald. I have lived without women. I'm ignorant of that type of pleasure. But I think that once you like even one woman, it's probable that you'll like others too!
OSVALD: And maybe cards and dubious company?
MANDERS: Osvald!
OSVALD: Sorry, pastor. I didn't mean to put you in a difficult position.
MANDERS: You *have* put me in a difficult position! And apart from that — watch what you say. You're talking about a dead man!
OSVALD: I don't want to judge him! But I have the right to know what kind of person he was!
MANDERS: A harmless man, I assure you. He never purposely did anyone any harm.
OSVALD: And what did my mother do? How did she endure it? What did she do to change it?
MANDERS: Luckily your mother has a strong character. She tried to control him, to protect him, and she more or less succeeded!
OSVALD: Perhaps in the end she succeeded only in oppressing him unbearably?
MANDERS: Your mother is an angel.
OSVALD: I saw him weeping.
MANDERS: Weeping?
OSVALD: Sobbing! Didn't you say my father was harmless?
MANDERS: Ask anyone you want, Osvald!
OSVALD: I've seen my mother sitting for hours in front of a mirror with the look of a madwoman on her face — her eyes strange.
MANDERS: Believe me, he was a harmless man! No, Osvald, you're making some mistake! Almost all couples have such problems.
OSVALD: You're not telling me the truth, pastor!
MANDERS: Then I don't know it!
OSVALD: So it seems.
MANDERS: Then why are you asking me?
OSVALD: I thought I would learn something! I would confirm something.
MANDERS: Confirm what, Osvald, your illusions?
OSVALD: Exactly, pastor! Illusions, ghosts, call them what you will! Listen to me. Of course they couldn't always quarrel in

whispers. I saw and heard things I couldn't understand at the time — but they frightened me — and because of that, I can still hear and see them. When I was growing up, I began to see it all, in bits and pieces. Like when you're in a dark room, and light is slowly coming in. The furniture, the pictures, the china, and silver begin to take shape. I fear, pastor, that they tormented each other, that their life was some kind of hell.

MANDERS: That's absolutely impossible. Your childish sensitivity magnified it all, as happ . . .

OSVALD: And my intuition? Is it wrong too?

MANDERS: What can I say? Anyway I think all these convoluted reflections that are so fashionable with you young people are not healthy.

OSVALD: The truth, you mean? Agh, pastor, I prefer it, whatever it is. Besides I've no time for embellishing it.

MANDERS: Why such melancholy, Osvald? You're so young. You want for nothing. Everyone here loves you. Tomorrow at the Opening they . . .

OSVALD: Tell me, pastor. Who had the idea for this institution? You?

MANDERS: No, not at all! Your mother. I, of course, helped her.

OSVALD: And this totally unsuitable name, who chose it?

MANDERS: Why unsuitable, Osvald? It was built with his estate. I don't see anything blameworthy!

OSVALD: I worship my mother, but this hypocrisy of hers infuriates me.

MANDERS: I ask you to consider what this institution means to the community.

OSVALD: It could have been built with her own estate. I'm an Alving! The normal thing would be for me to inherit from my father, not my mother!

MANDERS: Isn't it the same thing?

OSVALD: You see nothing behind this original idea?

MANDERS: No Osvald, I see nothing suspicious!

OSVALD: Agh, pastor, how you like to repair everything!

MANDERS (*naturally offended*): So I'm a repairman now! It doesn't matter! Anyway, if I may say so, these thoughts you have are sick!

OSVALD: But I am sick, Pastor Manders.

MANDERS: Then change your ideas. *They're* making you ill.

OSVALD: I didn't conjure them up out of nothing.

MANDERS: Yes, but you exaggerate and torment yourself without reason.

OSVALD: Perhaps I know something more.

MANDERS: About me?

OSVALD: No, why? What have you got to do with it? Do you know that she was always writing me letters, eulogizing my father and their beautiful life together?

MANDERS: Of course not. How would I know?

OSVALD: Would it have been so terrible for her to explain to me that they didn't get on? Their real guilt was their cowardice in not separating from the moment they saw that they were incompatible! What criminal cowardice! What kind of desert were they living in? Hadn't they even a trustworthy friend to advise them, to help them to separate? And now this institution, and in memory of... to remember what?

MANDERS (*comes forward and stands beside the* NIGHTWATCH-MAN): I'll have to interrupt here to tell you that I was already filled with premonitions! You know what they meant. On the very Opening Day, through a strange act of carelessness, all the buildings of the Orphanage were consumed by fire — and it was uninsured! And much, much worse: Osvald — he said something a short time before that, how could I know what he meant — Osvald was suffering from a serious form of syphilis, inherited from his father. He was reduced to a vegetative state. His own mother, Helena, had to... You know about that. I won't continue. Yes I had premonitions, but how could I have imagined I was talking to a young man who was dying! Otherwise, I would have thought more about what I was saying. (*He turns towards Osvald*): I'll give you some advice, Osvald, since as an older man, and a minister, I perhaps know a little more about life: Don't let your youthful ideas and sensibilities give you the wrong idea about what your poor parents did, and myself, and others. You called me a repairman! When you're my age, you'll realise that in the end we're all repairmen. (*He gives a forced laugh to mollify him.*)

OSVALD: I'll bear that in mind. I think I'll go for a walk before it gets dark.

MANDERS: And Osvald — enjoy yourself for as long as you're here. Leave everything else to time. That's the best advice of all.

OSVALD: Exactly. Only time has no reason to hurry just because *I* haven't very much of it left. Nor has our beautiful nature any

reason to concern herself, just because I have troubled thoughts. So *let's* allow time to sort it all out. And don't say anything to my mother, if you would be so good.
MANDERS: Of course not.
OSVALD: Thank you, pastor. Good evening to you.
(OSVALD *goes off.* MANDERS *is thoughtful, silent, motionless.*)
NIGHTWATCHMAN: Pastor.
MANDERS (*thoughtfully to himself*): Good evening, Osvald.
NIGHTWATCHMAN (*anxiously but restrainedly*): Pastor.
(MANDERS *turns and looks at him absentmindedly.*)
NIGHTWATCHMAN: Now that I know more I'll . . .
(*The* NIGHTWATCHMAN *pauses when he sees* MRS ALVING, *dressed in black, passing by in the background. She stops, as if sensing the presence of* MANDERS, *just as he also senses her presence. They speak to each other from a distance, without looking at each other. Their dialogue is fragmented, the phrases half-finished — like the tired remnants of a wind blowing after a storm.*)
MANDERS: I always used to go out. Now the distance is rather . . .
MRS ALVING: It's the same with everything.
MANDERS: Anyway, you shouldn't go out without an umbrella.
MRS ALVING: It's not raining now as it . . . It's not raining, no . . .
MANDERS: Indeed it was . . . a short while ago . . . not much though, but one never knows . . . one never . . .
MRS ALVING: Yes, perhaps. But it wasn't so heavy that . . . more like sleet.
MANDERS: And this cold wind.
MRS ALVING: Have you been here long?
MANDERS: Just in case, don't go too far.
MRS ALVING: I won't go now after all . . . just as far as the meteorite.
MANDERS: They say it didn't land only two centuries ago, but much earlier. The wind's really blowing hard out there . . . always blowing.
MRS ALVING: Nonsense . . . the leaves make you think so. Birch trees have strange foliage . . . restless.
MANDERS: They've cut a lot of them down, in the forest. There's . . .
MRS ALVING: When I was a child I used to think that every tree had its own wind that made the leaves . . .
MANDERS: Nathan, you know him . . . sorry, you asked me

something.
MRS ALVING: Did I? What about Nathan.
MANDERS: Nathan, yes . . . but what did you . . . ? I meant the one who works on the farms.
MRS ALVING: He'll be very old now.
MANDERS: He's well . . . yet he's still working.
MRS ALVING: So . . . how was he?
MANDERS: He's well. In the end, how very many years a man can live and work.
MRS ALVING: You were right. It's more like sleet.
MANDERS: I didn't say that.
MRS ALVING: Maybe *I* did. What does it matter?
MANDERS: Now I remember what I wanted to say to you. Yes, of course, we used to discuss it. Nathan would argue that winter was coming early . . . prematurely. "The geese have left already," he'd say. They migrate, you know. They go south, very far away . . . yes, indeed.
MRS ALVING: A sure sign. Are you here for long?
MANDERS: A few days. They wanted my advice on the extension.
MRS ALVING: I think *I* saw you the day before yesterday. You rarely see anyone on this road now. Only those who have land at the head of the fjord . . . rarely . . . I can see their footprints so clear on the ground. The same when I was a child . . . those footprints on a lonely road . . . lonely beyond too . . . isn't it?
MANDERS: Yes, indeed, such quiet! Now that you mention the extension . . . not going well. What can *I* say about it? But there's also the blessing on the harvest. It's very important for our farmers to have their hay in for the winter . . . God willing.
MRS ALVING: Why shouldn't He be?
MANDERS: So every birch has its own wind.
MRS ALVING: Yes . . . now they're — heavy with moisture with the sleet . . . They're not trembling, otherwise . . .
MANDERS: So it seems.
MRS ALVING: But in the spring and summer . . .
MANDERS: Of course . . .

(MRS ALVING *continues on her way.* MANDERS *and the* NIGHTWATCHMAN, *their attention turned towards her, are silent until she leaves.*)

NIGHTWATCHMAN: I was saying, now that I know more...
MANDERS: There's no need. I know less now — much less. Good night.

(MANDERS *goes off leaving the* NIGHTWATCHMAN *perplexed. He begins to carry the items he had brought on stage, out to the wings. Meanwhile the light slowly dims, and the stage becomes dark again.*)

—— THE END ——

APPENDIX

THREE ARTICLES

BY

LOUIS MUINZER

on the performance or rehearsed reading

of *The Four Legs of the Table*

and *Ibsenland*

These articles were published in Greek translation in the Athenian literary journal, *Themata Logotechnias* ("Kambanellis in Belfast" in vol. 2, March–June 1996, "A Kambanellis playreading in Belfast" and "Kambanellis visits Ibsen" in vol. 30, 2005). The original English texts submitted to the journal are published here for the first time.

KAMBANELLIS IN BELFAST

When they were founded almost twenty-five years ago, Belfast's Delphic Players chose a Greek name — one that, they hoped, would suggest the mysterious wisdom that is the life-blood of true Theatre, as opposed to the slick superficialities of plastic stagecraft. The first production of this new amateur group was also Greek — *Eumenides* by the Father of Tragedy, the great Aeschylus himself. In the quarter of a century since then, the Delphics have never attempted to dazzle Belfast, "the Athens of Ulster", with "safe" productions of popular West End and Broadway hits. Rather, they have simply tried to be worthy of their own Greek origins.

Along with a few classics by Molière, Ibsen and Aeschylus, the Delphics have attempted to open out the local dramatic repertory by performing contemporary plays that travel far beyond the precincts of "fashionable" and "trendy" productions. It is highly appropriate, therefore, that they explore the work of Aeschylus's successors. On May 27th, 1995, at the Lyric Players Theatre in Belfast, they began their exploration of Modern Greek drama with a rehearsed reading of *The Four Legs of the Table* by Iakovos Kambanellis.

The reading was made possible by the good will of the Lyric Players Theatre, who welcomed the opportunity to bring new European work to the attention of local theatre people and drama lovers alike. The setting for the venture — as for other Lyric readings in the past — was the theatre's upstairs foyer, which provided comfortable seating and a pleasantly informal atmosphere for those who attended the event. For the Delphics, this was a far more inviting space than that provided by the Lyric's main auditorium — a pleasant space, but one rather large and formal for a friendly play-reading.

More important than the attractions of the reading space, of course, was the quality of the script held in the hands of the Delphic readers. In that, they were extremely fortunate, for the Kambanellis text they used was the work of a talented and resourceful translator, Marjorie Chambers. The Delphics found her English script fluent and effective, and they enjoyed working with it. Indeed, they consider Marjorie Chambers to be a considerable asset to the Ulster theatre scene: every vital theatrical community depends on the presence and participation of translators like her, just as it depends on the creative work of actors, directors and designers.

In her work on the Kambanellis play, Marjorie Chambers was

assisted by her son Michael, who acted as her dialogue adviser, and who attended Delphic rehearsals to give the group his highly intelligent support.

Ten members of the Delphic Players participated in the reading of *The Four Legs of the Table* before a Saturday-morning audience that included several prominent Belfast theatre people. Kambanellis has been called Greece's most distinguished living dramatist, and his "black comedy" about the wealthy family headed by an ancient, but seemingly immortal "papa", will undoubtedly be well known to the Greek readers of this article. Nevertheless, both play and playwright were *terra incognita* to most of the people in the Belfast audience. Indeed, save for certain individuals who had studied Modern Greek under Marjorie Chambers herself, few had probably ever heard of the eminent Greek dramatist: they came with an open mind to "see what he was like".

In their attempt to judge Kambanellis, the audience found its attention sorely tried at one point by the sounds of an audience leaving an event in the Lyric's main auditorium — a distraction due to a misunderstanding about interval timing at the busy Lyric, and in no way the fault of the helpful staff. The sound, naturally enough, subsided, but some of the Delphics feared that Kambanellis's spell had been broken, and that the reading had lost its cohesion and drive. The incident is worth mentioning, however, not as a calamity but as a triumph for the Greek dramatist. Not only did the power of the play survive "off-stage" distraction, it scored as great a success with its audience as any comparable event the present writer can recall. At the end, the response was strong and enthusiastic. Not everyone present may remember the wonderfully exotic name of Iakovos Kambanellis, but they will remember his talent and his play!

Besides its own humour, satiric bite and humanity, *The Four Legs of the Table* probably owes some of its Belfast success to its unexpected affinity with Irish drama. One member of the audience, Ms Roma Tomelty, spotted that quality immediately. Like many important Irish plays, the Kambanellis work is a family drama, a play about the members of a nuclear social group. Ms Tomelty, herself an actress, writer and director, has a special reason for stressing this, for she is the daughter of dramatist Joseph Tomelty, whose *All Souls' Night* is not only one of the classics of the Ulster theatre, but also a family play that would bear interesting comparison to Kambanellis's. To be sure, the Tomelty piece is darker and highly tragic, and his humble family from the coast of County Down has not risen socially and economically like its Greek counterpart in *The Four Legs of the Table*. Nevertheless, the underlying folk-stock is there, and the powerful sense of family relationships.

Indeed, when the brothers and sisters in the Kambanellis play throw off their affluence and begin doing an earthy Greek dance, we are in the world of another Northern play — *Dancing at Lughnasa* by Brian Friel. Like Tomelty's family from County Down, Friel's poor sisters from Donegal will never "make it big" like Alice, Kostas and their five brothers and sisters in *The Four Legs of the Table,* but the same rich European peasant blood dances in them all — and they dance with it. At bottom, the Kambanellis family simply represents the New Society that is smothering the rich, earthy stock of both Greece and Ireland. Aeschylus would know what to say about that — he would ask his chorus to utter one long-drawn, tragic cry of lament.

All in all, then, Marjorie Chambers has opened a new door connecting Belfast theatre and that of Greece, and standing in that doorway is the figure of Iakovos Kambanellis. Now, *The Four Legs of the Table* deserves a full-scale production in English, to see if it can work its magic in true theatrical conditions. The only practical difficulties lie in cast size (ten), and in the special nature of the play's distinctive roles. Appealing as the play is, it might be no easy matter to collect enough talented *middle-aged* performers to play the members of the play's large Greek family effectively. For a rehearsed reading, the Delphic players could, with some difficulty, muster a full company, but several of the talented Delphic actors were simply too young to be completely effective in a full production. Much of the blackness of this comedy lies in the incongruous immaturity of a stageful of ageing characters who should be "old enough to know better". Young actors in the cast would blunt both the play's humour and its satire.

But there is no gainsaying the fact that *The Four Legs of the Table* is a compelling play with considerable local appeal: a play that makes strong contact with Belfast people. Of course, with its witty exploration of the ineptitude of society's economic elite, the work also has international appeal. Greek? Undoubtedly! . . . But Kambanellis is a bit of a Celt at heart . . .

LOUIS MUINZER

A KAMPANELLIS PLAYREADING IN BELFAST

A rehearsed reading of *Ibsenland* by Iakovos Kambanellis was presented by Translators' Theatre at Belfast's Lyric Players Theatre, on the afternoon of Saturday, May 30, 1998. Translators' Theatre is a small, new group formed to promote the translation of foreign plays by Northern Ireland linguists with an interest in good drama. The Kambanellis reading featured the work of one of the province's most talented and experienced play translators, Marjorie Chambers. The readers taking part in the performance were members of the Delphic Players, who were joined for the occasion by several other actors.

As I was involved in the preparation of the reading, my personal views are naturally rather biased! However, if the readers will make allowance for my role in the proceedings, I shall be happy to share my responses with them.

First of all, however, I need not worry about bias when I say that all of us involved in the performance liked Mr Kambanellis's play very much indeed. It is a work of psychological depth, tense character interaction and effective dramatic structuring. We also felt to a man — and to a woman — that Marjorie Chambers' English text read very well indeed: the dialogue was fluent, the idiom sharp and the movement of the text carried Kambanellis's drama forward without a single stumble. To our ears, the play read as if it were actually written in English. As a translator myself, I well know how difficult it is to achieve such naturalness of expression. Having recently read a painfully distracting translation of a play by another notable European dramatist, I can say without hesitation that Iakovos Kambanellis is blessed with a very talented translator in Marjorie Chambers.

As *Ibsenland* uses Henrik Ibsen's *Ghosts* as its point-of-departure, the play held a special fascination for me. Working in collaboration with the Irish dramatist John Boyd, I had translated that very play for staging by the Lyric Theatre some years earlier. In conversation during our Kambanellis rehearsal and after the reading itself, a number of people commented how effectively the language of the script harmonized with that of Ibsen's own play. I certainly agree with that, but what personally impressed me even more was Kambanellis's fidelity to Ibsen's characters themselves. In his treatement of Pastor Manders, the dramatist moved beneath the surface of Ibsen's great portrait of a flawed human being and brought his psychological findings out onto the stage. Anything the Greek dramatist adds to the Norwegian's portrait is consistent and effective both as character interpretation and theatre. I found this creative bond between two playwrights separated by a century and situated on the opposite borders of Europe most impressive indeed — and it is not a theatrical fellow-feeling that an audience should take for granted: I know an Italian continuation of another Ibsen masterpiece that loses contact entirely with the original and ultimately imposes a quite alien attitude upon it. The fault does not lie, of course, in the fact that the later dramatist was Italian, but that he had too little creative "feeling" for the Norwegian master and his view of mankind. No one can say that of Kambanellis!

The reading itself proved to be a very surprising personal experience for me. Due to everyone's hectic schedule, we were able to spend only one morning in rehearsing our presentation, before returning after a quick lunch to "perform" before the audience. After we had sat down together and read through the script once, I found that there was insufficient time for a second complete run-through. So that we could do our best in these trying circumstances, I decided to focus on certain short segments of the script for which simple movement could be worked out; this piecemeal work would at least visually enhance our presentation. The result was a set of disjointed "bits and pieces" that should have meant little dramatically. However, I was aware that by some inexplicable magic, Kambanellis's characters had come to life, even in this fragmentary second run-through! Far from worrying that we had failed to do the play justice through lack of rehearsal time, I felt a sudden and complete confidence in our treatment of the script. I went off to lunch with the cast without a worry in the world.

When we returned for the reading, the audience responded much as I thought they would: they were impressed by a coherent and moving evocation of a worthy new play. I myself, however, was understandably distracted: to me, the reading looked like the beginning of an actual production that could be worked up and staged in short order! As the rest of the audience attended to the actual reading, I was far ahead of them, relating in my imagination the treatment before me to a "finished" production.

My only regret is that the commitments of the group do not seem to make that dream production of *Ibsenland* possible. Indeed, Matthew Faris, who played Pastor Manders with great conviction and thereby anchored the entire performance, is a professional actor and, naturally, does not appear in actual productions with amateurs like us in the Delphic Players. Also, young Marty Rea, our moving Osvald, is training to become a professional actor and should not be distracted from his studies at this time. However, both of those talented performers took with them a definite faith in the Kambanellis play and its translation. Both will tell others in the profession about it and try to arouse interest in its production.

Along with the two guest performers just mentioned, the Delphic Players themselves displayed a strong commitment to the play and gave powerful, humane voices to Kambanellis's characters. Our experienced actresses Denise McGeown and Zelda Clegg played the younger and older Mrs Alving respectively, Matthew Tourney was the young Manders and newcomer Bill Smith was *Ibsenland's* humane and quizzical Nightwatchman. It was a token of the spirit and group-feeling of the Delphics that Mary Tourney, one of our most talented performers, was happy to assist in preliminary work and to play a supporting role as the reader of the dramatist's Foreword. My only regret is that the dramatist himself could not be with us to share the experience of his play in English. If he had been, he would have understood more intimately the strong ties between Greek and Irish theatre and recognized, too, the growing affection that we Delphics feel for the land that gave us our theatre, those long, long centuries ago.

LOUIS MUINZER

KAMBANELLIS VISITS IBSEN

While attending the 1998 Ibsen Festival in Oslo (August 27–September 5), I encountered an old theatrical friend — No, it was not *Peer Gynt* or *Brand* or *Rosmersholm*, although all three of those Norwegian masterpieces were present, too. Indeed, the friend met so unexpectedly in Norway was Greek, not Scandinavian, and was in fact *Ibsenland* by Iakovos Kambanellis. When I had first encountered the play in the preceding May, it was visiting Belfast, Northern Ireland, for a rehearsed reading by Translators' Theatre. At that time, I had been greatly impressed by the work in Marjorie Chambers' fluent English translation, so I was pleased to renew my acquaintance in Norway-this time under production conditions and in the original Greek.

As a fresh exploration of certain characters in Ibsen's *Ghosts*, the Kambanellis play is a work to engross all who admire Ibsen's powerful tragedy. Its action takes place on an almost deserted stage at the end of a run of Ibsen's own play. The theatre's night-watchman questions the actor who played Pastor Manders about that character, and as they talk the actor becomes the clergyman once more and relives his relationship to Mrs. Alving, the loving and deeply lovable woman he rejected. This exploration is presented dramatically in a series of moving scenes, which portray the pair both as potential lovers in their youth and as isolated and unfulfilled individuals in their lonely maturity. Throughout, the Greek writer rejects the lead of some modern playwrights who use Ibsen material as the springboard for their own, quite different dramatic conceptions: Kambanellis's treatment of Manders and Mrs Alving seems to me noteworthy for its fidelity to Ibsen's fundamental approach to those characters. *Ibsenland* honours Henrik Ibsen by occupying the Norwegian master's own dramatic landscape.

While the production possibilities of the Kambanellis script struck me forcefully at the Belfast reading, my full assessment of the work came in Oslo, where *Ibsenland* rose before me in a full-scale professional production. The play was performed at the Ibsen Festival by Piramatiki Skini of Thessalonica in the Norwegian National Theatre's Amfi Scene, the smaller, more intimate and flexible of its two major auditoriums. Although I was unable to understand a word of the Greek dialogue — alas! — I *was* able to follow the production without undue difficulty and to judge its effectiveness to my personal satisfaction. Without exaggeration, I can say that the production more than fulfilled my hopes. Movingly directed by Petros Zivanos and performed by a talented cast, *Ibsenland* was one of my viewing highpoints at the 1998 Ibsen Festival.

Before attending the Oslo performance, I had seen only one play in Modern Greek. That, too, had its strength and drive, but it was a rather intellectual performance that by its nature lacked great warmth. However, it was precisely its warmth and its moving immediacy that most impressed me about Piramatiki Skini's *Ibsenland*. Other companies, I suppose, might have staged this play with power and effectiveness, but few, surely, could have caught so compellingly its web of compassion, apartness and final anguish as well as these Thessalonicans. If this production is characteristic of their work, I should like to see more of it.

Ironically enough, the emotional content of the production was at least partially focused by the treatment of the one character in the play who had no role in the drama *per se*: the Nightwatchman. Playing this unobtrusive character, Nikos Litras brought a caring and curious presence to the performance that focused and helped humanize its central action. Besides serving as an intermediary between the characters and the audience, he may also have embodied the probing spirit of *Ibsenland*'s two dramatic artists: of Iakovos Kambanellis, the Greek who wrote it, and of Henrik Ibsen, the Norwegian who planted its seeds.

Within the performance that the Nightwatchman and the audience experienced, the almost painful humanity of the play was powerfully developed in the scenes between the young Manders and the girl who became Mrs Alving. As the inhibited young clergyman and the sweetheart he never had, Yannis Mochlas and Kiriaki Matsakidou gave performances that live in my memory for their radiant but deeply painful innocence; they were lovers who talked from the two sides of a psychological wall of young Manders' making. In the scenes exploring this pair, Kambanellis was "out on his own" as a dramatist, for they have no counterparts in *Ghosts,* and the two young actors played them flawlessly.

As Ibsen's ill-fated Osvald, Dimitris Sakatzis brought the youth of the two lovers into the world of the older, unfulfilled people they so tragically became. Those failed lovers themselves were played by a pair of performers capable of transmitting great emotional power, Dimitris Naziris and Eti Stamouli.

As both Pastor Manders and the actor who had played that role in *Ghosts,* Naziris gave one of the most moving performances in the 1998 Ibsen Festival. A passionate actor capable of clear, but rapid-fire delivery, he caught much of the play's mood of baffled anguish and provided its strongest drive. Indeed, it was his powerful response to the probing of the Watchman that generated the drama itself and set it moving towards its powerful ending. Poignantly played by Ms Stamouli and Naziris, the two failed lovers finally stand alone on stage, speaking with powerful feeling from within their isolation. It was a scene worthy of the Norwegian master himself, but to me it seemed closer to Chekhov than Ibsen. Whatever its theatrical antecedents may be, however, it was my favourite scene in the entire Ibsen Festival programme.

But good as the cast of *Ibsenland* may have been, their already-strong performance was enhanced by the contribution of a talented actor who didn't appear on stage at all: designer Ioanna Manoledaki. I call Ms Manoledaki an "actor", for her powerful setting was not simply there as a backdrop, but was a vital performance in its own right, conditioning the action as if it were visual dialogue. As that action took place in a theatre at the end of a *Ghosts* production, one would expect the Ibsen setting itself to be depicted here in partially stripped-down form.

Ms. Manoledaki, however, rejected the obvious and created a poetic, indeed elegiac, milieu for *Ibsenland* — a milieu of mirror reflections dominated by a giant pair of glasses, with one of its earpieces broken.

Like all evocative theatrical symbols, Ioanna Manoledaki's spectacles bore as many shades of meaning as there were seats in the National's Amfi Scene. For me, they were above all the glasses actually worn in the play by the young Manders, but magnified for dramatic emphasis: they were the transparent barricades before his eyes as he looked outward at the girl he should have fulfilled. But they were worn by the audience, too, and represented the sad, inadequate means of vision through which we look at one another and just stand watching. And were they not also the lenses of Kambanellis's own sadness as his script looks out at the people of his world?

Although the water pipe controlling the effect had accidentally been turned off at the performance I attended, those huge glasses actually could weep! But they hardly needed to do so to make their point: do we not all weep inwardly at the waste of love epitomized by both *Ibsenland* and *Ghosts*?

To director Petros Zivanos, his actors and his production team, I offer my congratulations and send along no negative criticisms of their work. I also congratulate Iakovos Kambanellis for providing Oslo audiences with a drama of humanity and power. However, I do have a single question that refuses to go away.

My question is this: Can *Ibsenland* stand alone and grip an audience that lacks prior knowledge of Ibsen's own play? It happens that another Ibsen-based new play was performed at the 1998 festival, but this did not involve Ibsen's own characters and simply used an Ibsen drama as background. This play, *Austria* by the Norwegian dramatist Cecilie Loveid, explored the philosopher Ludwig Wittgenstein, who spent much time in Norway and whose personality suggests parallels with that of Ibsen's Brand. There is no doubt in my mind that the Loveid work can be staged elsewhere with complete independence, aided perhaps by a good programme note on the Ibsen connection. But what of *Ibsenland*, with its intimate and powerful relation to *Ghosts*? Can it be successfully performed out of its Ibsen context? The piece is so moving that I suspect that its power can carry it through. However, it is difficult for me to judge that, for besides co-translating the play personally, I have seen *Ghosts* in English, Norwegian, Czech and Hebrew, and I came to the new Greek play already steeped in Ibsen's. An experienced arts worker who attended our Belfast reading suggested that *Ghosts* and *Ibsenland* might be effectively presented together in appropriate sequence, and that would certainly be an ideal arrangement. In any case, *Ibsenland* represents a fine achievement and must not be forgotten!

LOUIS MUINZER